CGP has National 5 Physics covered!

SQA National 5 Physics is no walk in the park... but with this brilliant
CGP book, revising will be a picnic. So pack some sandwiches.

It's packed with crystal-clear study notes and exam-style questions — and because
we're revision experts, you can be sure it covers everything you need to know. Perfect.

How to access your free Online Edition

This book includes a free Online Edition to read on your PC, Mac or tablet.
To access it, just go to **cgpbooks.co.uk/extras** and enter this code...

2443 3672 4291 7049

By the way, this code only works for one person. If somebody else has used
this book before you, they might have already claimed the Online Edition.

CGP — the best by miles! ☺

Our sole aim here at CGP is to produce the highest quality books —
carefully written, immaculately presented and dangerously close to being funny.

Then we work our socks off to get them out to you
— at the cheapest possible prices.

Contents

Scientific Skills
The Scientific Method 2
Communication & Issues Created by Science 3
Designing Investigations 4
Collecting Data 6
Processing Data 7
Processing and Presenting Data 8
Units and Equations 10
Drawing Conclusions 11
Uncertainties and Evaluations 12

Section 1 — Dynamics
Scalars and Vectors 13
Resultant Vectors 14
Speed and Velocity 15
Acceleration 16
Measuring Motion 17
Velocity-Time Graphs 18
Forces 19
Newton's First and Second Laws 20
Newton's Third Law 21
Weight, Mass and Gravity 22
Terminal Velocity 23
Energy and Work Done 24
Kinetic and Potential Energy 25
Projectile Motion 26
More Projectile Motion and Satellites 27
Revision Questions for Section 1 28

Section 2 — Space
Our Solar System, Our Galaxy and the Universe 29
Origin of the Universe 30
Observing the Universe 31
Satellites 32
Challenges and Risks of Space Travel 33
More Challenges and Risks of Space Travel 34
Mechanics of Space Travel 35
Revision Questions for Section 2 36

Section 3 — Electricity
Charge and Electric Fields 37
Electrical Current and Circuit Symbols 38
Potential Difference and Resistance 39
Investigating Components 40
Circuit Devices 41
More Circuit Devices 42
Series Circuits 43
Parallel Circuits 44
Potential Dividers 45
Transistors 46
Mains Electricity 47
Power 48
Revision Questions for Section 3 49

Section 4 — Properties of Matter
The Kinetic Model and Temperature 50
Specific Heat Capacity 51
Specific Latent Heat 52
Pressure 53
Gas Laws — Boyle's Law 54
Gas Laws — Gay-Lussac's Law 55
Gas Laws — Charles' Law and The Ideal Law 56
Revision Questions for Section 4 57

Section 5 — Waves
Wave Properties 58
Wave Speed 59
Diffraction 60
Electromagnetic Waves and Refraction 61
Sources and Uses of EM Waves 62
More Sources and Uses of EM Waves 63
Revision Questions for Section 5 64

Section 6 — Radiation

Nuclear Radiation...65
Activity and Half-Life..66
Determining Half-Life..67
Medical Uses of Ionising Radiation..................68
More Uses of Ionising Radiation.....................69
Background Radiation and Risk.......................70
Radiation Dose..71
Comparing Radiation Dose...............................72
Nuclear Fission..73
Nuclear Fusion...74
Revision Questions for Section 6....................75

Performing Experiments

Apparatus and Techniques................................76
Working with Electronics...................................78

Answers..79
Index...81

Published by CGP

From original material by Richard Parsons.

Editors: Emily Garrett, Sharon Keeley-Holden, Hannah Taylor, Charlotte Whiteley
Contributors: Rebecca Cornwell, Paddy Gannon, Chris Rossi, Malcolm Thomson

With thanks to Ian Francis and Karen Wells for the proofreading.
With thanks to Jan Greenway for the copyright research.

ISBN: 978 1 78294 993 0

Data in table on page 72 contains public sector information licensed under the Open Government Licence v3.0.
http://www.nationalarchives.gov.uk/doc/open-government-licence/version/3/

Printed by Elanders Ltd, Newcastle upon Tyne.
Clipart from Corel®

Text, design, layout and original illustrations © Coordination Group Publications Ltd (CGP) 2018

All rights reserved.

Photocopying more than one section of this book is not permitted, even if you have a CLA licence.
Extra copies are available from CGP with next day delivery • 0800 1712 712 • www.cgpbooks.co.uk

The Scientific Method

This section isn't about how to 'do' science — but it does show you the way most scientists work.

Scientists Come Up With Hypotheses — Then Test Them

1) Scientists try to explain things. They start by observing something they don't understand.
2) They then come up with a hypothesis — a possible explanation for what they've observed.
3) The next step is to test whether the hypothesis might be right or not. This involves making a prediction based on the hypothesis and testing it by gathering evidence (i.e. data) from investigations. If evidence from experiments backs up a prediction, you're a step closer to figuring out if the hypothesis is true.

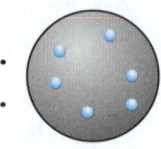

About 100 years ago, scientists hypothesised that atoms looked like this.

Several Scientists Will Test a Hypothesis

1) Normally, scientists share their findings in peer-reviewed journals, or at conferences.
2) Peer-review is where other scientists check results and scientific explanations to make sure they're 'scientific' (e.g. that experiments have been done in a sensible way) before they're published. It helps to detect false claims, but it doesn't mean that findings are correct — just that they're not wrong in any obvious way.
3) Once other scientists have found out about a hypothesis, they'll start basing their own predictions on it and carry out their own experiments. They'll also try to reproduce the original experiments to check the results — and if all the experiments in the world back up the hypothesis, then scientists start to think the hypothesis is true.
4) However, if a scientist does an experiment that doesn't fit with the hypothesis (and other scientists can reproduce the results) then the hypothesis may need to be modified or scrapped altogether.

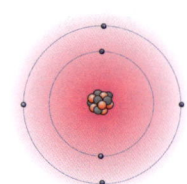

After more evidence was gathered, scientists changed their hypothesis to this.

If All the Evidence Supports a Hypothesis, It's Accepted — For Now

1) Accepted hypotheses are often referred to as theories. Our currently accepted theories are the ones that have survived this 'trial by evidence' — they've been tested many times over the years and survived.
2) However, theories never become totally indisputable fact. If new evidence comes along that can't be explained using the existing theory, then the hypothesising and testing is likely to start all over again.

Now we think it's more like this.

Theories Can Involve Different Types of Models

Scientists test models by carrying out experiments to check that the predictions made by the model happen as expected.

1) A representational model is a simplified description or picture of what's going on in real life. Like all models, it can be used to explain observations and make predictions. E.g. the kinetic model is a simplified way of describing how particles in matter behave (see p.50). It can be used to explain the properties of solids, liquids and gases.
2) Computational models use computers to make simulations of complex real-life processes. You can use a computational model to simulate nuclear decay (p.67). They're used when there are a lot of different variables (factors that change) to consider, and because you can easily change their design to take into account new data.
3) All models have limitations on what they can explain or predict. E.g. the Big Bang model (p.30) can be used to explain why everything in the Universe is moving away from us. One of its limitations is that it doesn't explain the moments before the Big Bang.

I'm off to the zoo to test my hippo-thesis...

The scientific method has developed over time, and many people have helped to develop it. From Aristotle to modern day scientists, lots of people have contributed. And many more are likely to contribute in the future.

Communication & Issues Created by Science

Scientific developments can be great, but they can sometimes raise more questions than they answer...

It's Important to Communicate Scientific Discoveries to the General Public

Some scientific discoveries show that people should change their habits, or they might provide ideas that could be developed into new technology. So scientists need to tell the world about their discoveries.

> Radioactive materials are used widely in medicine for imaging and treatment (see p.68). Information about these materials needs to be communicated to doctors so they can make use of them, and to patients, so they can make informed decisions about their treatment.

Scientific Evidence can be Presented in a Biased Way

1) Reports about scientific discoveries in the media (e.g. newspapers or television) aren't peer-reviewed.
2) This means that, even though news stories are often based on data that has been peer-reviewed, the data might be presented in a way that is over-simplified or inaccurate, making it open to misinterpretation.
3) People who want to make a point can sometimes present data in a biased way. (Sometimes without knowing they're doing it.) For example, a scientist might overemphasise a relationship in the data, or a newspaper article might describe details of data supporting an idea without giving any evidence against it.

Scientific Developments are Great, but they can Raise Issues

Scientific knowledge is increased by doing experiments. And this knowledge leads to scientific developments, e.g. new technologies or new advice. These developments can create issues though. For example:

Economic issues: Society can't always afford to do things scientists recommend (e.g. investing in space exploration) without cutting back elsewhere.

Social issues: Decisions based on scientific evidence affect people — e.g. should alcohol be banned (to prevent health problems)? Would the effect on people's lifestyles be acceptable...?

Personal issues: Some decisions will affect individuals. For example, someone might support the use of nuclear power stations, but object if one was built near to where they live.

Environmental issues: Human activity often affects the natural environment — e.g. radioactive tracers can be used to detect leaks in underground pipes (p.69) — but these could cause environmental problems if the tracer leaked out into the soil.

Science Can't Answer Every Question — Especially Ethical Ones

1) We don't understand everything. We're always finding out more, but we'll never know all the answers.
2) In order to answer scientific questions, scientists need data to provide evidence for their hypotheses.
3) Some questions can't be answered yet because the data can't currently be collected, or because there's not enough data to support a theory.
4) Eventually, as we get more evidence, we'll answer some of the questions that currently can't be answered, e.g. what the impact of global warming on sea levels will be. But there will always be the "Should we be doing this at all?"-type questions that experiments can't help us to answer...

> Think about new drugs which can be taken to boost your 'brain power'.
> - Some people think they're good as they could improve concentration or memory. New drugs could let people think in ways beyond the powers of normal brains.
> - Other people say they're bad — they could give you an unfair advantage in exams. And people might be pressured into taking them so that they could work more effectively, and for longer hours.

Tea to milk or milk to tea? — Totally unanswerable by science...

Science can't tell you whether or not you should do something. That's for you and society to decide. But there are tonnes of questions science might be able to answer, like where life came from and where my superhero socks are.

Scientific Skills

Designing Investigations

Dig out your lab coat and dust down your badly-scratched safety goggles... it's investigation time. You need to know how to plan and carry out investigations. But before we get into the ins and outs of what makes a good experiment, let's talk about safety...

Investigations Can be Hazardous

1) A hazard is something that could potentially cause harm.
2) Hazards from science experiments might include:

   - Lasers, e.g. if a laser is directed into the eye, this can cause blindness.
   - Gamma radiation, e.g. gamma-emitting radioactive sources can cause cancer.
   - Fire, e.g. an unattended Bunsen burner is a fire hazard.
   - Electricity, e.g. faulty electrical equipment could give you a shock.

Investigations include experiments and studies.

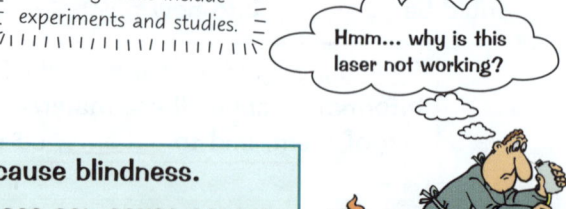

Hmm... why is this laser not working?

3) Part of planning an investigation is making sure that it's safe.
4) You should always make sure that you identify all the hazards that you might encounter. Then you should think of ways of reducing the risks from the hazards you've identified. For example:

   - If you're working with springs, always wear safety goggles. This will reduce the risk of the spring hitting your eye if the spring snaps.
   - If you're using a Bunsen burner, stand it on a heat proof mat. This will reduce the risk of starting a fire.

You can find out about potential hazards by looking in textbooks, doing some internet research, or asking your teacher.

An Investigation Must Have an Aim

1) Before you begin any investigation, you need to have an aim.
2) An aim should clearly describe the purpose of your investigation. For example:

   Aim: To investigate how the angle of a ramp affects a trolley's acceleration down it.

Investigations Produce Evidence to Support or Disprove a Hypothesis

1) Scientists observe things and come up with hypotheses to explain them (see p.2). The investigations you do will be based on the same principle. For example:

   Observation: People have big feet and spots.
   Hypothesis: Having big feet causes spots.

2) To determine whether or not a hypothesis is right, you need to do an investigation to gather evidence. To do this, you need to use the hypothesis to make a prediction — something you think will happen that you can test. E.g. people with bigger feet will have more spots.

3) Investigations are used to see if there are patterns or relationships between two variables, e.g. to see if there's a pattern or relationship between the variables 'number of spots' and 'size of feet'.

Scientific Skills

Designing Investigations

Evidence Needs to be Reliable and Valid

1) Data is reliable if it is repeatable and reproducible. Scientists are more likely to have confidence in reliable data.
2) Repeatable means that if the same person does an experiment again using the same methods and equipment, they'll get similar results.
3) Reproducible means that if someone else does the experiment, or a different method or piece of equipment is used, the results will still be similar.
4) Valid results are both repeatable and reproducible and they answer the original question. They come from experiments that were designed to be a fair test (see below).

Controlling Variables Improves Validity

1) A variable is something that has the potential to change, e.g. mass. In a lab experiment you usually change one variable and measure how it affects another variable.

> Example: you might change only the mass of a toy car travelling down a ramp and measure how this affects its average speed.

2) To make it a fair test, everything else that could affect the results should stay the same — otherwise you can't tell if the thing you're changing is causing the results or not.

> Example continued: you need to keep the angle of the ramp the same, otherwise you won't know whether any change in average speed is caused by the change in angle of the ramp or the difference in mass of the car.

Part of designing an investigation includes choosing the most appropriate apparatus and techniques to measure or control your variables — see pages 76-78.

3) The variable you **CHANGE** is called the **INDEPENDENT** variable.
4) The variable you **MEASURE** is called the **DEPENDENT** variable.
5) The variables that you **KEEP THE SAME** are called **CONTROL** variables.

> Example continued:
> Independent variable = mass of toy car
> Dependent variable = average speed of toy car
> Control variables = angle of ramp, position of car release, material on ramp etc.

6) Because you can't always control all the variables, you often need to use a **CONTROL EXPERIMENT** — an experiment that's kept under the same conditions as the rest of the investigation, but doesn't have anything done to it. This is so that you can see what happens when you don't change anything at all.

This is no high street survey — it's a designer investigation...

Planning an investigation is tricky business — you need to make sure that you've thought of everything in order for your method to give you valid results. And, not only do you need to be able to plan your own investigations, you should also be able to look at someone else's plan and decide whether or not it needs improving. Remember, whoever's plan you're thinking about, always consider any potential hazar... oof, sorry, I tripped.

Scientific Skills

Collecting Data

You've designed the perfect investigation — now it's time to get your hands mucky and collect some data.

Your Data Should be Reliable, Accurate and Precise

1) Reliable results are repeatable and reproducible, see previous page.
2) To check repeatability you need to repeat the readings and check that the results are similar. You need to repeat each reading at least three times.
3) To make sure your results are reproducible you can cross check them by taking a second set of readings with another instrument (or a different observer).
4) Your data also needs to be ACCURATE. Really accurate results are those that are really close to the true answer. The accuracy of your results usually depends on your method — you need to make sure you're measuring the right thing and that you don't miss anything that should be included in the measurements. E.g. estimating the instantaneous acceleration of a cart down a slope by measuring the time with a stopwatch isn't very accurate because this will not take into account your reaction time. It's more accurate to measure the time using light gates or video analysis (see p.17).
5) Data also needs to be PRECISE. Precise results are ones where the data is all really close to the mean (average) of your repeated results (i.e. not spread out).

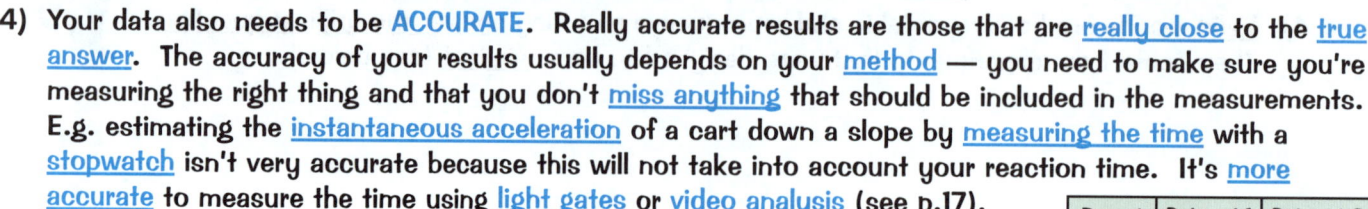

Repeat	Data set 1	Data set 2
1	12	11
2	14	17
3	13	14
Mean	13	14

Data set 1 is more precise than data set 2.

Brian's result was a curate.

Your Equipment has to be Right for the Job

1) The measuring equipment you use has to be sensitive enough to measure the changes you're looking for. For example, if you need to measure changes of 1 cm³ you need to use a measuring cylinder that can measure in 1 cm³ steps — it'd be no good trying with one that only measures in 10 cm³ steps.
2) The smallest change a measuring instrument can detect is called its RESOLUTION. E.g. some mass balances have a resolution of 1 g, some have a resolution of 0.1 g, and some are even more sensitive.
3) Also, equipment needs to be calibrated by measuring a known value. If there's a difference between the measured and known value, you can use this to correct the inaccuracy of the equipment.

You Need to Look out for Errors and Anomalous Results

1) The results of your experiment will always vary a bit because of RANDOM ERRORS — unpredictable differences caused by things like human errors in measuring. E.g. the errors you make when reading from a ruler are random. You have to estimate or round the distance when it's between two marks — so sometimes your figure will be a bit above the real one, and sometimes it will be a bit below.
2) You can reduce the effect of random errors by taking repeat readings and finding the mean. This will make your results more precise.
3) If a measurement is wrong by the same amount every time, it's called a SYSTEMATIC ERROR. For example, if you measured from the very end of your ruler instead of from the 0 cm mark every time, all your measurements would be a bit small. Repeating the experiment in the exact same way and calculating a mean won't correct a systematic error.
4) Just to make things more complicated, if a systematic error is caused by using equipment that isn't zeroed properly, it's called a ZERO ERROR. For example, if a mass balance always reads 1 gram before you put anything on it, all your measurements will be 1 gram too heavy.
5) You can compensate for some systematic errors if you know about them though, e.g. if your mass balance always reads 1 gram before you put anything on it you can subtract 1 gram from all your results.
6) Sometimes you get a result that doesn't fit in with the rest at all. This is called an ANOMALOUS RESULT. You should investigate it and try to work out what happened. If you can work out what happened (e.g. you measured something totally wrong) you can ignore it when processing your results.

If there's no systematic error, then doing repeats and calculating a mean can make your results more accurate.

Watch what you say to that mass balance — it's very sensitive...

Weirdly, data can be really precise but not very accurate. For example, a fancy piece of lab equipment might give results that are really precise, but if it's not been calibrated properly those results won't be accurate.

Scientific Skills

Processing Data

Processing your data means doing some calculations with it to make it more useful. But you need to make sure you're happy using significant figures and scientific notation before doing any calculations.

Data Needs to be Organised

Tables are dead useful for organising data. When you draw a table use a ruler and make sure each column has a heading (including the units).

You Might Have to Find the Average

1) When you've done repeats of an experiment you should always calculate the mean (a type of average). To do this add together all the data values and divide by the total number of values in the sample.

Ignore anomalous results when calculating the mean.

EXAMPLE: The results of an experiment show the extension of a spring when a force is applied to it. Calculate the mean of the extension for the spring.

Repeat 1 (cm)	Repeat 2 (cm)	Repeat 3 (cm)	Mean (cm)
18	26	22	(18 + 26 + 22) ÷ 3 = 22

2) You might also need to calculate the median or mode (two more types of average). To calculate the median, put all your data in numerical order — the median is the middle value. The number that appears most often in a data set is the mode.

If you have an even number of values, the median is halfway between the middle two values.

Be Aware of Significant Figures in Calculations

The first significant figure of a number is the first digit that's not zero. The second and third significant figures come straight after (even if they're zeros).

1) For your final answer, you should round to the lowest number of significant figures (s.f.) given.
2) Remember to write down how many significant figures you've rounded to after your answer.
3) If your calculation has multiple steps, only round the final answer, or it won't be as accurate.

EXAMPLE: A motor transfers 2.4 J of energy in 0.715 s. Calculate the power of the motor.
Power = $E \div t$ = 2.4 J ÷ 0.715 s = 3.3566... = 3.4 W (2 s.f.) — Final answer should be rounded to 2 s.f.
2 s.f. / 3 s.f.

See p.48 for more on power.

You Might Need to Work With Numbers in Scientific Notation

1) Sometimes in physics it's useful to write numbers in scientific notation (sometimes called standard form).
2) This is where you change very big or small numbers with lots of zeros into something more manageable, e.g. 0.017 can be written 1.7×10^{-2}.
3) To do this you just need to move the decimal point left or right.
4) Numbers in scientific notation always look like this: $A \times 10^n$

A is always a number between 1 and 10.

n is the number of places the decimal point has moved. It's positive if the decimal point has moved left, and negative if it's moved right.

EXAMPLE: A wave has a wavelength of 0.0025 m. Write this figure in scientific notation.
1) The first number needs to be between 1 and 10 so the decimal point needs to move after the '2'.
2) Count how many places the decimal point has moved — this is the power of 10. Don't forget the minus sign because the decimal point has moved right.

0.0025
2.5×10^{-3}

My physics teacher called me average — how mean...

It can be tough to get the hang of scientific notation — practise writing really big and little numbers to get used to it.

Scientific Skills

Processing and Presenting Data

Presenting your data correctly is a super important part of science. It's time to look at how you can present your results in a nice chart or graph to help you spot any patterns in your data.

Bar Charts Can be Used to Show Different Types of Data

Bar charts can be used to display:

1) Categoric data — data that comes in distinct categories, e.g. solid, liquid, gas.
2) Discrete data — data that can be counted in chunks, where there's no in-between value, e.g. number of nuclear decays is discrete because you can't have half a nuclear decay.
3) Continuous data — numerical data that can have any value within a range, e.g. length, volume.

There are some golden rules you need to follow for drawing bar charts:

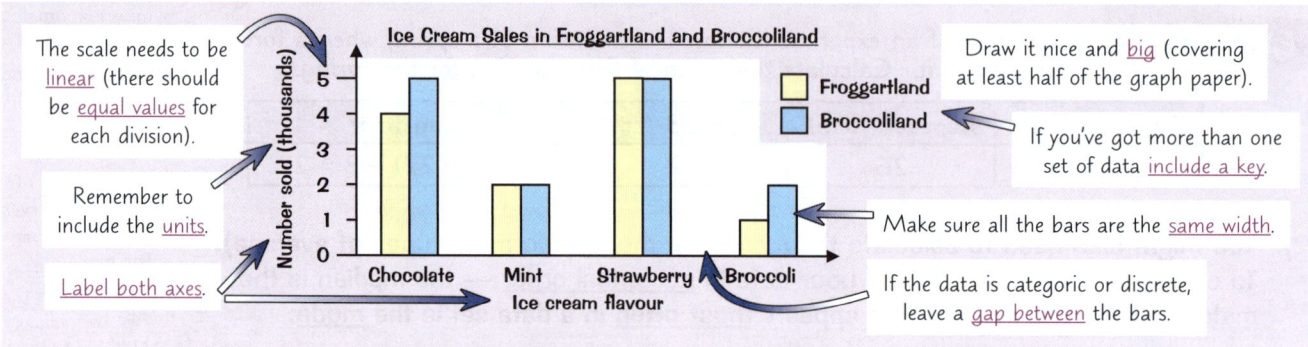

- The scale needs to be linear (there should be equal values for each division).
- Remember to include the units.
- Label both axes.
- Draw it nice and big (covering at least half of the graph paper).
- If you've got more than one set of data include a key.
- Make sure all the bars are the same width.
- If the data is categoric or discrete, leave a gap between the bars.

Scatter or Line Graphs Can be Used to Plot Continuous Data

If both variables are continuous you can use a scatter graph to show if there is a relationship between them.

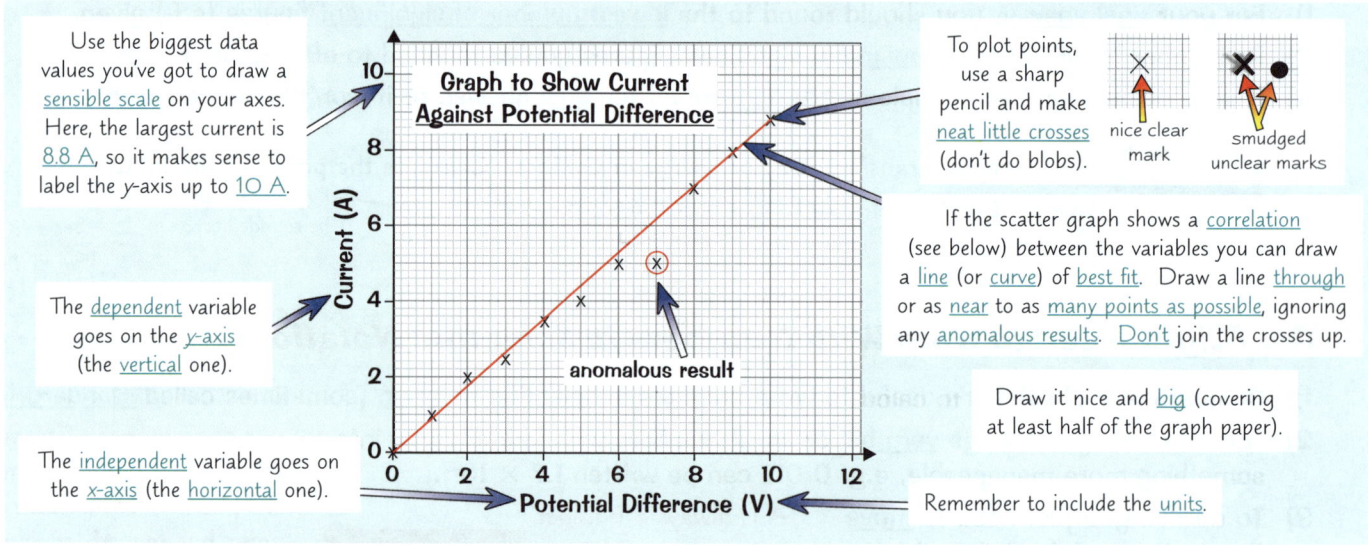

- Use the biggest data values you've got to draw a sensible scale on your axes. Here, the largest current is 8.8 A, so it makes sense to label the y-axis up to 10 A.
- The dependent variable goes on the y-axis (the vertical one).
- The independent variable goes on the x-axis (the horizontal one).
- To plot points, use a sharp pencil and make neat little crosses (don't do blobs). nice clear mark / smudged unclear marks
- If the scatter graph shows a correlation (see below) between the variables you can draw a line (or curve) of best fit. Draw a line through or as near to as many points as possible, ignoring any anomalous results. Don't join the crosses up.
- Draw it nice and big (covering at least half of the graph paper).
- Remember to include the units.

A line graph is normally used if you're plotting how a variable changes with time. The only difference is that, in a line graph, the points are normally joined up by a line or curve.

Graphs Show the Relationship Between Two Variables

1) You can get three types of correlation (relationship) between variables:
2) Just because there's correlation, it doesn't mean the change in one variable is causing the change in the other — there might be other factors involved (see page 11).

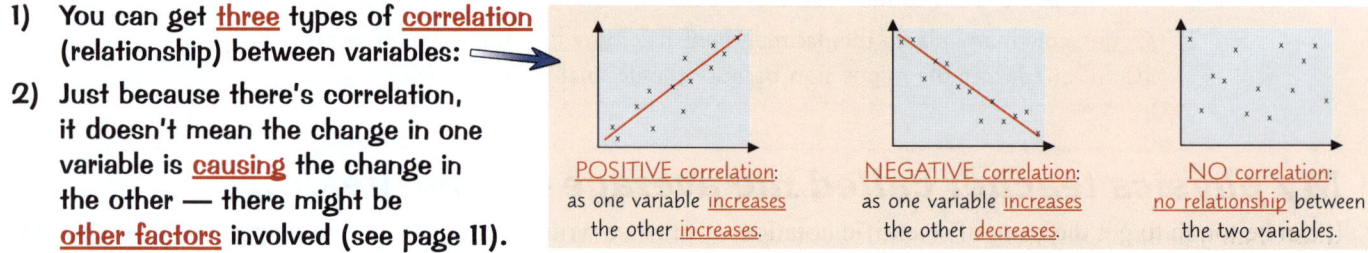

POSITIVE correlation: as one variable increases the other increases.

NEGATIVE correlation: as one variable increases the other decreases.

NO correlation: no relationship between the two variables.

Scientific Skills

Processing and Presenting Data

Graphs Can Give You a Lot of Information About Your Data

1) The gradient (slope) of a graph tells you how quickly the dependent variable changes if you change the independent variable:

$$\text{gradient} = \frac{\text{change in } y}{\text{change in } x}$$

This graph shows the distance travelled by a vehicle against time. The graph is linear (it's a straight line graph), so you can simply calculate the gradient of the line to find out the speed of the vehicle.

1) To calculate the gradient, pick two points on the line that are easy to read and a good distance apart.
2) Draw a line down from one of the points and a line across from the other to make a triangle. The line drawn down the side of the triangle is the change in y and the line across the bottom is the change in x.

Change in y = 6.8 − 2.0 = 4.8 m
Change in x = 5.2 − 1.6 = 3.6 s

Speed = gradient = $\frac{\text{change in } y}{\text{change in } x} = \frac{4.8 \text{ m}}{3.6 \text{ s}} = $ 1.3 ms^{-1}

The units of the gradient are (units of y)(units of x)$^{-1}$.

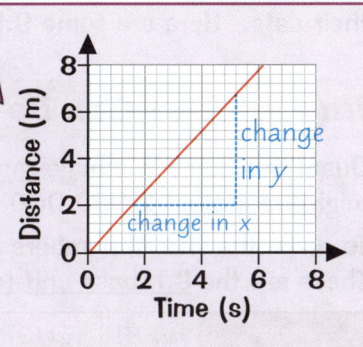

You can use this method to calculate other rates from a graph, not just the rate of change of distance (which is speed). Just remember that a rate is how much something changes over time, so x needs to be the time.

2) The intercept of a graph is where the line of best fit crosses one of the axes. The x-intercept is where the line of best fit crosses the x-axis and the y-intercept is where it crosses the y-axis.

You can Find the Gradient of a Curved Graph by Drawing a Tangent

1) If a graph is curved, you can find the gradient at a certain point by drawing a tangent to the curve at that point. Then you find the gradient of the tangent.
2) A tangent is a line that is parallel to the curve at that point.

This graph shows a distance-time graph. You can use the graph to calculate the speed at a certain time, e.g. at 25 s by finding the gradient of the line at that point:

1) To calculate the gradient at 25 s, draw a tangent to the curve at 25 s (red line).
2) Calculate the gradient of the tangent (blue lines) using the method for straight lines above.

Change in y = 90 − 10 = 80 m
Change in x = 26 − 16 = 10 s

Speed = gradient = $\frac{\text{change in } y}{\text{change in } x} = \frac{80 \text{ m}}{10 \text{ s}} = $ 8 ms^{-1}

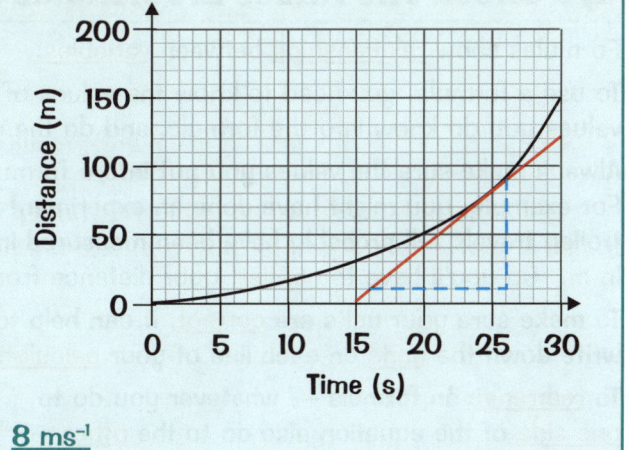

I saw my physics teacher on holiday — he was a tanned gent...

Lots of nifty graph skills here. Gradients aren't too hard, but make sure those tangents don't trip you up.

Scientific Skills

Units and Equations

Graphs and maths skills are all very well, but the numbers don't mean much if you can't get the <u>units</u> right.

S.I. Units Are Used All Round the World

1) It wouldn't be all that useful if I defined volume in terms of <u>bath tubs</u>, you defined it in terms of <u>egg-cups</u> and my pal Sarwat defined it in terms of <u>balloons</u> — we'd never be able to compare our data.
2) To stop this happening, scientists have come up with a set of <u>standard units</u>, called S.I. units, that all scientists use to measure their data. Here are some S.I. units you'll see in physics:

Quantity	S.I. Base Unit
mass	kilogram, kg
length	metre, m
time	second, s
temperature	kelvin, K

Scaling Prefixes Can Be Used for Large and Small Quantities

1) Quantities come in a huge <u>range</u> of sizes. For example, the volume of a swimming pool might be around 2 000 000 000 cm³, while the volume of a cup is around 250 cm³.
2) To make the size of numbers more <u>manageable</u>, larger or smaller units are used. These are the <u>S.I. base unit</u> (e.g. metres) with a <u>prefix</u> in front:

prefix	tera (T)	giga (G)	mega (M)	kilo (k)	deci (d)	centi (c)	milli (m)	micro (µ)	nano (n)
multiple of unit	10^{12}	10^9	1 000 000 (10^6)	1000	0.1	0.01	0.001	0.000001 (10^{-6})	10^{-9}

3) These <u>prefixes</u> tell you <u>how much bigger</u> or <u>smaller</u> a unit is than the base unit. So one <u>kilometre</u> is <u>one thousand</u> metres.

The conversion factor is the number of times the smaller unit goes into the larger unit.

4) To <u>swap</u> from one unit to another, all you need to know is what number you have to divide or multiply by to get from the original unit to the new unit — this is called the <u>conversion factor</u>.

- To go from a <u>bigger unit</u> (like m) to a <u>smaller unit</u> (like cm), you <u>multiply</u> by the conversion factor.
- To go from a <u>smaller unit</u> (like g) to a <u>bigger unit</u> (like kg), you <u>divide</u> by the conversion factor.

5) Here are some conversions that'll be useful in physics:

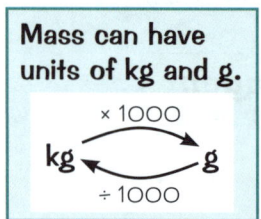
Mass can have units of kg and g.

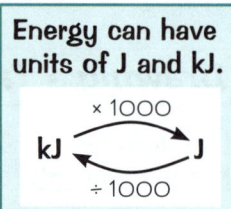
Energy can have units of J and kJ.

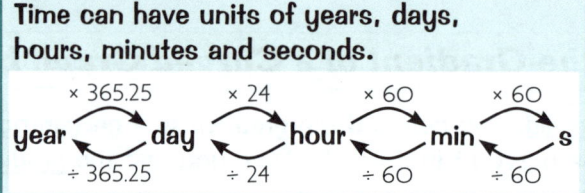
Time can have units of years, days, hours, minutes and seconds.

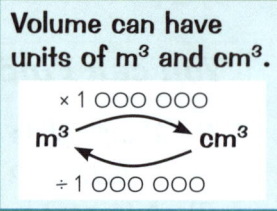
Volume can have units of m³ and cm³.

Always Check The Values in Formulas Have the Right Units

1) Formulas show <u>relationships</u> between <u>variables</u>.
2) To use a formula, you need to know the values of <u>all but one</u> of the variables. <u>Substitute</u> the values you do know into the formula, and do the calculation to work out the final variable.
3) Always make sure the values you put into a formula have the <u>right units</u>. For example, you might have done an experiment to find the speed of a trolley. The distance the trolley travels will probably have been measured in cm, but the equation to find speed uses distance in m. So you'll have to <u>convert</u> your distance from cm to m before you put it into the equation.
4) To make sure your units are <u>correct</u>, it can help to write down the <u>units</u> on each line of your <u>calculation</u>.
5) To <u>rearrange</u> an formula — whatever you do to <u>one side</u> of the equation also do to the <u>other</u>.

> wave speed = frequency × wavelength.
> You can <u>rearrange</u> this formula to find the <u>frequency</u> by <u>dividing each side</u> by wavelength to give: frequency = wave speed ÷ wavelength.

I wasn't sure I liked units, but now I'm converted...

It's easy to get in a muddle when converting between units, but there's a handy way to check you've done it right. If you're moving from a smaller unit to a larger unit (e.g. g to kg) the number should get smaller, and vice versa.

Scientific Skills

Drawing Conclusions

Congratulations — you're nearly at the end of a gruelling investigation, time to draw conclusions.

You Can Only Conclude What the Data Shows and NO MORE

1) Drawing conclusions might seem pretty straightforward — you just look at your data and say what pattern or relationship you see between the dependent and independent variables.

The table on the right shows the potential difference across a light bulb for three different currents through the bulb:

Current (A)	Potential difference (V)
6	4
9	10
12	13

CONCLUSION: As the current through the bulb increases, the potential difference across the bulb increases.

2) But you've got to be really careful that your conclusion matches the data you've got and doesn't go any further. ⟶ You can't conclude that the potential difference across any circuit component will be higher for a larger current — the results might be completely different.

3) You also need to be able to use your results to justify your conclusion (i.e. back up your conclusion with some specific data). ⟶ The potential difference across the bulb was 9 V higher with a current of 12 A compared to a current of 6 A.

4) When writing a conclusion you need to refer back to the original aim: ⟶ The aim of this experiment might have been to investigate the effect of current through a filament bulb on the potential difference across it. When writing your conclusion, refer back to this aim.

Correlation DOES NOT Mean Cause

If two things are correlated (i.e. there's a relationship between them) it doesn't necessarily mean a change in one variable is causing the change in the other. There are three possible reasons for a correlation:

1) CHANCE: It might seem strange, but two things can show a correlation purely due to chance.

   For example, one study might find a correlation between people's hair colour and how good they are at frisbee. But other scientists don't get a correlation when they investigate it — the results of the first study are just a fluke.

2) LINKED BY A 3RD VARIABLE: A lot of the time it may look as if a change in one variable is causing a change in the other, but it isn't — a third variable links the two things.

   For example, there's a correlation between water temperature and shark attacks. This isn't because warmer water makes sharks crazy. Instead, they're linked by a third variable — the number of people swimming (more people swim when the water's hotter, and with more people in the water you get more shark attacks).

3) CAUSE: Sometimes a change in one variable does cause a change in the other. You can only conclude that a correlation is due to cause when you've controlled all the variables that could, just could, be affecting the result.

   For example, there's a correlation between smoking and lung cancer. This is because chemicals in tobacco smoke cause lung cancer. This conclusion was only made once other variables (such as age and exposure to other things that cause cancer) had been controlled and shown not to affect people's risk of getting lung cancer.

I conclude that this page is a bit dull...

...although, just because I find it dull doesn't mean that I can conclude it's dull (you might think it's the most interesting thing since that kid got his head stuck in the railings near school). In the exam you could be given a conclusion and asked whether some data supports it — so make sure you understand how far conclusions can go.

Scientific Skills

Uncertainties and Evaluations

Hurrah! The end of another investigation. Well, now you have to work out all the things you did wrong.

Uncertainty is the Amount of Error Your Measurements Might Have

1) Uncertainty is a measure of how confident you are that your results are correct.
2) When you repeat a measurement, you often get a slightly different figure each time you do it due to random error (p.6). This means that each result has some uncertainty to it.
3) The measurements you make will also have some uncertainty in them due to limits in the resolution of the equipment you use (see page 6).
4) You can reduce the uncertainty by taking repeats and calculating a mean, and by using equipment with a higher resolution.
5) Measuring a greater amount of something helps to reduce uncertainty. For example, in a speed experiment, measuring the distance travelled over a longer period compared to a shorter period will reduce the percentage uncertainty in your results.

Evaluations — Describe How it Could be Improved

An evaluation is a critical analysis of the whole investigation.

1) You should comment on the method — was it valid? Did you control all the other variables to make it a fair test?
2) Comment on the quality of the results — was there enough evidence to reach a valid conclusion? Were the results repeatable, reproducible, accurate and precise?
3) Were there any anomalous results? If there were none then say so. If there were any, try to explain them — were they caused by errors in measurement? Were there any other variables that could have affected the results? You should comment on the level of uncertainty in your results too.
4) All this analysis will allow you to say how confident you are that your conclusion is right.
5) Then you can suggest any changes to the method that would improve the quality of the results, so that you could have more confidence in your conclusion. For example, you might suggest changing the way you controlled a variable, or increasing the number of measurements you took. Taking more measurements at narrower intervals could give you a more accurate result. For example:

> Radioactive isotopes have a half-life (the time taken for their activity to halve). Say you use several identical samples of an isotope to do an experiment to find the half-life of the isotope. If you take readings of the activity after 1, 2, 3, 4 and 5 minutes, and from the results see that the half-life is somewhere between 4 and 5 minutes, you could then repeat the experiment with one of the other samples, taking more measurements between 4 and 5 minutes to get a more accurate value for the half-life.

6) You could also make more predictions based on your conclusion, then further experiments could be carried out to test them.

When suggesting improvements to the investigation, always make sure that you say why you think this would make the results better.

Evaluation — next time, I'll make sure I don't burn the lab down...

Well, hopefully you'll have enough scientific skills now to do some awesome investigations. But remember, it's not just in the lab that you'll need your scientific skills knowledge — you can be asked about it in the exam.

Scientific Skills

Section 1 — Dynamics

Scalars and Vectors

The stuff on this page is pretty darn important. Learn it, don't forget it, and do the question at the end.

Scalars are Just Numbers, but Vectors Have Direction Too

1) Everything you measure in physics is either a scalar quantity, or a vector quantity.
2) Scalar quantities are just numbers — they simply tell you the 'size' (or 'magnitude') of the thing you're measuring, and nothing more.
3) Mass is a scalar quantity, as it only has a size. Other scalar quantities include: ⇨ **Scalar quantities:** speed, distance, time, energy, etc.
4) Vector quantities tell you both the size of the thing AND its direction.
5) Force is a vector quantity, because it is applied in a particular direction, e.g. 10 N to the right. Other vector quantities include: ⇨ **Vector quantities:** velocity, displacement, acceleration, etc.
6) Vectors are usually represented by an arrow — the length of the arrow shows the magnitude, and the direction of the arrow shows the direction of the quantity.

> When we use vectors, we talk about there being a positive and a negative direction. E.g. a force applied in one direction could be a force of 10 N, but if it were applied in the opposite direction it would be a force of –10 N. In either direction the size of the force is 10 N. You can often pick a positive direction that makes the calculations easier.

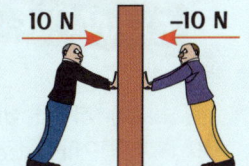

The Motion of an Object can be Described in Three Ways

1) A moving object can be described by its speed, direction of travel and whether its speed is changing.
2) Distance, displacement, speed and velocity are all terms used to describe an object's motion.

Distance is Scalar, Displacement is a Vector

1) Distance is a scalar quantity, its symbol is *d*. It's how far an object has travelled.
2) Displacement is a vector quantity, its symbol is *s*. It measures the net distance and direction in a straight line from an object's starting point to its finishing point — e.g. the plane flew 5 metres north. The direction could be relative to a point, e.g. towards the school, or a bearing (a three-digit angle measured clockwise from north) e.g. 035°.
3) If you walk 5 m north, then 5 m south, your displacement is 0 m but the distance travelled is 10 m.

Speed and Velocity are Both How Fast You're Going

1) Speed is a scalar quantity and velocity is a vector quantity. Both have the symbol *v*.

   ms⁻¹ means m/s or metres per second.

   > Speed is how fast the object's going (e.g. 30 mph or 20 ms⁻¹) with no regard to the direction. Velocity is speed of the object in a given direction, (e.g. 30 mph north or 20 ms⁻¹, 060°).

2) This means you can have objects travelling at a constant speed with a changing velocity. This happens when an object is changing direction whilst staying at the same speed. An object moving in a circle at a constant speed has a constantly changing velocity, as the direction is always changing (e.g. a car going around a roundabout).

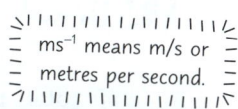

A fairly easy way to start the section... — wait, whose cat is this?
Important things to know in life: how to correctly pronounce 'scone' and the difference between scalars and vectors.
Q1   Describe the difference between scalar and vector quantities.   [1 mark]

Resultant Vectors

Scale drawings and trigonometry are useful things — they can help you work out resultant vectors.

You can Add Vectors to Find the Resultant

1) Adding two or more vectors is called finding the resultant of them. Whatever the quantity is — displacement, force, velocity — the procedure is the same.
2) If the vectors all act along the same line (they're all parallel), the resultant vector is found by adding those going in one direction and subtracting any going in the opposite direction.
3) E.g. if you walk 10 m north and then 6 m south, your resultant displacement is 10 − 6 = 4 m north.
4) Adding vectors together that aren't along the same line is a bit more tricky.
5) There are two methods you can use. Whatever method you choose, you always start by drawing a diagram with the vectors 'tip-to-tail'.

You can Find the Resultant of Vectors at Right Angles by Using Trigonometry

You can find the resultant of two vectors at right angles using Pythagoras and trigonometry.

EXAMPLE: Jemima goes for a walk. She walks 3.0 m north and 4.0 m east. Find the magnitude and direction of her displacement.

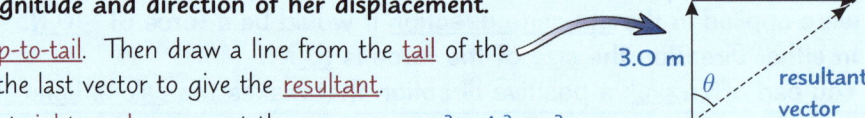

1) First, draw the vectors tip-to-tail. Then draw a line from the tail of the first vector to the tip of the last vector to give the resultant.
2) Because the vectors are at right angles, you get the magnitude of the resultant, R, using Pythagoras.
   $a^2 + b^2 = c^2$
   $R^2 = 3.0^2 + 4.0^2 = 25.0$
   So $R = \sqrt{25.0} = 5.0$ m
3) Using trigonometry, you know the opposite and the adjacent sides, so you can use $\tan\theta = $ opposite ÷ adjacent.
   $\tan\theta = (4.0 \div 3.0)$
   So $\theta = \tan^{-1}(4.0 \div 3.0) = 53.13...$
4) $\tan^{-1}$ means inverse tan — there's a button for it on your calculator.
5) Give the direction.
   So direction = 053° (to 2 s.f.)

You Can Use Scale Drawings to Find Any Resultant Vector

1) Draw all the vectors acting on an object, 'tip-to-tail', making sure they are to scale.
2) Then draw a straight line from the start of the first vector to the end of the last vector — this is the resultant vector.
3) Measure the length of the resultant vector on the diagram to find the magnitude of the vector and the angle to find the direction of the vector.

EXAMPLE: A raft is floating down a river which has a velocity of 3.0 ms⁻¹ north. It is being paddled with a velocity of 2.0 ms⁻¹ east. Find the magnitude and direction of the raft's resultant velocity.

1) Start by drawing a scale drawing of the vectors.
2) Make sure you choose a sensible scale (e.g. 1 cm = 1 ms⁻¹).
3) Draw the resultant from the tail of the first arrow to the tip of the last arrow.
4) Measure the length of the resultant velocity with a ruler and use the scale to find the magnitude.
5) Use a protractor to measure the direction as a bearing.

2 cm   1 cm = 1 ms⁻¹
3 cm   Resultant velocity
34°   3.6 cm = 3.6 ms⁻¹
Resultant velocity is 3.6 ms⁻¹ on a bearing of 034°.

You could also have said 34° clockwise from north — as long as the direction is clear.

Don't blow things out of proportion — it's only scale drawings...

Diagrams make most vector questions easier, so always start with one. Then get to work.

Q1 A toy boat crosses a stream. The boat moves with a velocity of 12 ms⁻¹ north. The river flows with a velocity of 5 ms⁻¹ west. Find the magnitude of the resultant velocity of the boat. [2 marks]

Section 1 — Dynamics

Speed and Velocity

Time for a quick recap on speed. You should race through this page. On your marks...

You can Find Speed or Velocity using Distance or Displacement and Time

1) Speed and velocity both measure how fast you're going, but speed is a scalar and velocity is a vector (p.13).
2) To find the speed or velocity (v) of an object at a constant speed or velocity, you need the distance covered (d) or the total displacement (s) over a period of time:

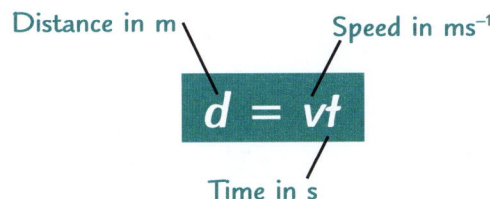
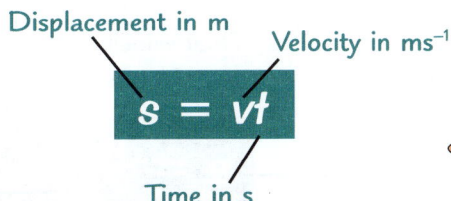

EXAMPLE: A cat skulks 20 m in 50 s. Find: a) its speed, b) how long it takes to skulk 32 m.

1) You'll need the equation for speed, distance and time. $d = vt$
2) Substitute the values you know and rearrange to find speed, v. $20 = v \times 50$
   So $v = 20 \div 50 = 0.4$ ms^{-1}
3) Now that the speed has been calculated, you can find the time, t, taken to travel a different distance at the same speed. $32 = 0.4 \times t$ so $t = 32 \div 0.4 = 80$ s

Moving Objects have Instantaneous and Average Speeds

1) Objects rarely travel at a constant speed or velocity. E.g. when you walk, run or travel in a car, your speed is always changing.
2) When the speed of an object is constantly changing, you can either talk about the average speed over a period of time or the instantaneous speed (the speed of an object at a particular moment). You can have instantaneous and average velocities too.
3) You can calculate the average speed or velocity ($\bar{v}$) with formulas similar to the ones above:

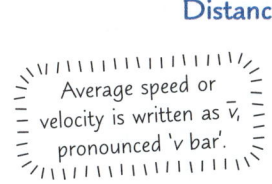
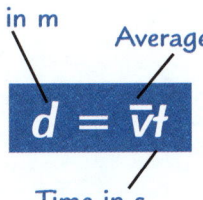
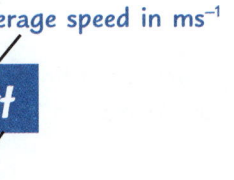
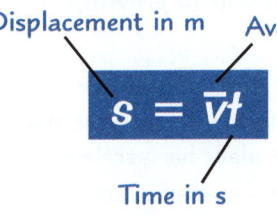
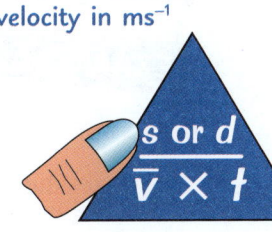

Average speed or velocity is written as $\bar{v}$, pronounced 'v bar'.

EXAMPLE: A tortoise travels for 12 s. His final displacement is 60 m. Calculate his average velocity.

1) The question gives you displacement and time, and asks you to work out average velocity. Write the correct equation for this. $s = \bar{v}t$
2) Substitute in the numbers and rearrange the equation for average velocity. $60 = \bar{v} \times 12$
   So $\bar{v} = 60 \div 12 = 5$ ms^{-1}

I feel the need, the need for calculating speed...

Average speed and instantaneous speed are totally different, make sure you understand the difference.

Q1 A person walks at 1.0 ms^{-1} for 10.0 s. They then speed up and walk at a speed of 1.5 ms^{-1} for 8.0 s. The total distance travelled by the person is 22 m.
   a) State the person's instantaneous speed at 5 s. [1 mark]
   b) Calculate the person's average speed over this journey. [3 marks]

Acceleration

Uniform acceleration sounds fancy, but it's just speeding up (or slowing down) at a constant rate.

Acceleration is the Rate of Change of Velocity

1) Acceleration is how quickly the velocity is changing.
2) This change in velocity can be a CHANGE IN SPEED or a CHANGE IN DIRECTION or both.
3) You can find the average acceleration of an object using:

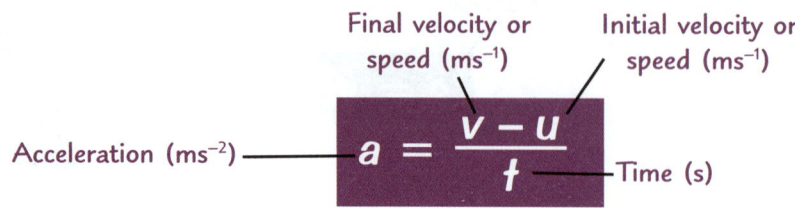

$$a = \frac{v - u}{t}$$

- Acceleration (ms^{-2})
- Final velocity or speed (ms^{-1})
- Initial velocity or speed (ms^{-1})
- Time (s)

An object travelling in a circle at a constant speed has a changing velocity (because it's always changing direction p.13), so it's always accelerating.

Initial velocity is just the starting velocity of the object.

4) Acceleration is a vector, like velocity — it can have a positive or negative value. If an object has a negative acceleration, it is either slowing down (decelerating), or speeding up in the negative direction.

Uniform Acceleration Means a Constant Acceleration

1) Constant acceleration is sometimes called uniform acceleration.
2) Acceleration due to gravity (g) can be assumed to be uniform for objects in free-fall. It's roughly equal to $9.8\ ms^{-2}$ near the Earth's surface and has the same value as gravitational field strength (p.22).
3) You can use the equation above for uniform acceleration (including acceleration due to gravity).

Remember, if the acceleration isn't constant then the equation gives the average acceleration.

EXAMPLE: A cyclist is in a race. As she approaches the finish line, she accelerates uniformly to increase her speed from 11 ms^{-1} to 15 ms^{-1} in 25 s. Calculate her acceleration.

Substitute into the acceleration equation.
$a = (v - u) \div t$
$= (15 - 11) \div 25 = 0.16\ ms^{-2}$

When the cyclist crosses the finish line, she immediately applies her brakes, and decelerates uniformly to come to a stop after 3 s. Calculate her acceleration after she crosses the finish line.

The cyclist comes to a stop, so the final speed is 0 ms^{-1}.
$a = (v - u) \div t$
$= (0 - 15) \div 3 = -5\ ms^{-2}$

Uniform problems — get a clip-on tie or use the equation above...

Don't mix up initial speed and final speed (or velocity), or else your answers will turn out all wrong.

Q1 A ball is dropped from a height. The speed of the ball just before it hits the ground is 14.7 ms^{-1}. Calculate the time taken for the ball to hit the ground from when it was dropped.
(acceleration due to gravity = 9.8 ms^{-2}) [3 marks]

Section 1 — Dynamics

Measuring Motion — PRACTICAL

Here's a simple experiment you can try out to measure average and instantaneous speed and acceleration.

You can Investigate the Motion of a Trolley on a Ramp with Light Gates

1) A light gate is a device that sends a beam of light (or sometimes infrared, see p.62) from one side of the gate to a detector on the other side. When something passes through the gate, the beam of light is interrupted. A light gate connected to a data logger can measure how long the beam was undetected.

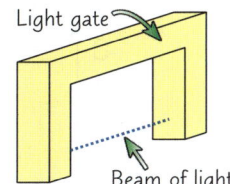

2) Set up your apparatus as shown in the diagram.
3) Before starting, measure the width of the card, and the distance between the two light gates.
4) Let the trolley roll down the ramp through the light gates.
5) The light gates and data logger will measure the time at which the card passes through each gate and how long it takes to pass through.

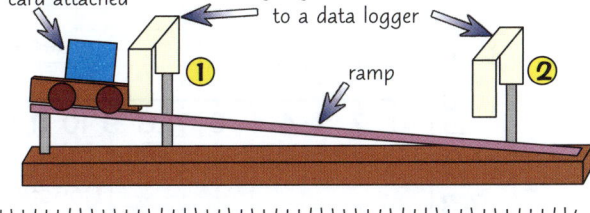

6) Light gates are appropriate for the tiny time intervals involved, and a centimetre ruler should be used for the distances. See p.76-77 for more on measuring times and distances.

If you connect your data logger to a computer, you'll probably be able to input the length of the interrupting card and distance between gates to get the computer to work out speeds and accelerations.

7) You can use your data to find the trolley's average and instantaneous speeds and accelerations:
   - You can calculate the instantaneous speed at each light gate. The distance the trolley travels whilst blocking the light signal in each light gate is equal to the card width. Divide this distance by the time taken to pass through a gate to work out the instantaneous speed at that gate ($v = d \div t$ — p.15).
   - For average speed between gates, divide the distance between the gates by the time taken to travel between them ($\bar{v} = d \div t$).
   - You can use $a = \frac{v - u}{t}$ (p.16) to calculate the trolley's average acceleration between the gates — u is the speed at the first light gate, v is the speed at the second light gate and t is the time taken to travel between them.
   - You can find the instantaneous acceleration at a light gate using a double interrupt card: The card blocks the light signal twice as it passes through a light gate. This means you can work out two instantaneous speeds (u and v) that are only a fraction of a second (t) apart. Then use $a = \frac{v - u}{t}$ to find the acceleration as the trolley passes through the light gate.
8) For a flat ramp like the one shown, the acceleration will be constant so the instantaneous and average acceleration will be equal (assuming that there's no friction, see p.23). But if the acceleration is changing (e.g. the ramp gradient changes), make sure you're always talking about the right quantity.

Video Analysis Software is an Alternative to Light Gates

1) Record a video of the object's motion beside a metre ruler and use video analysis software to view it frame by frame.

A frame is one of the many still images that make up the video.

2) Pick a point on the ruler and count how many frames the object takes to travel past it.
3) Divide the number of frames by the frame rate (number of frames per second) of the video to get the time taken for the object to travel past the point. Use $v = d \div t$ to find the instantaneous speed at that point (d is the length of the object).
4) You can do the same to find the average speed between two points. Count the number of frames the object takes to travel between the two points (d is the distance between the points).

If you want to investigate motion you'll need to invest in gates...

Learn how to measure average and instantaneous speed and acceleration, it could come up on the exam.

Q1 Explain how the average speed of an object can be found using two light gates. [3 marks]

Section 1 — Dynamics

Velocity-Time Graphs

Time for some velocity-time graphs, you lucky thing. These are brilliant for describing the motion of an object.

Velocity-Time (v-t) Graphs can be Used to Find Acceleration

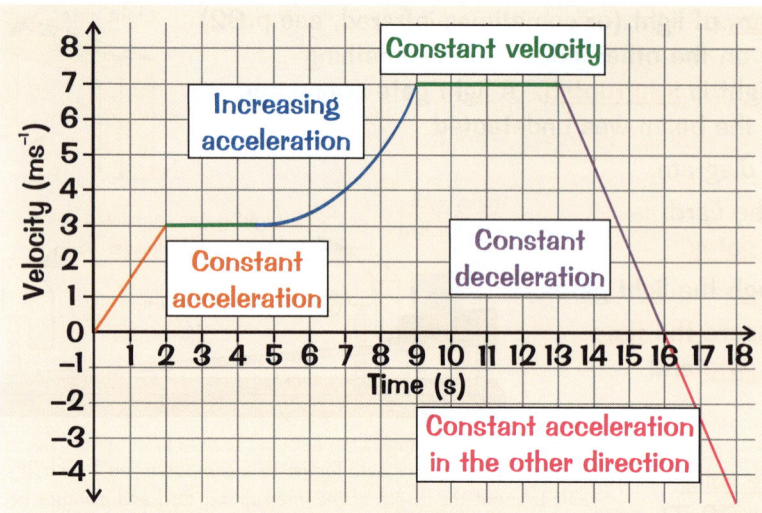

- Gradient of a v-t graph = acceleration (a).
- Flat sections represent constant (steady) velocity.
- The steeper the graph, the greater the acceleration or deceleration.
- Uphill sections (/) are acceleration.
- Downhill sections (\) are deceleration.
- A straight line means constant acceleration.
- A curve means changing acceleration.
- A line below the time axis means the object is moving in the other direction (negative velocity).

- You can calculate the acceleration at a point by finding the gradient of the tangent at that point (p.9).
- A speed-time graph is similar to a velocity-time graph, but on a speed-time graph the direction of motion isn't considered. You can still find the acceleration of the object by finding the gradient of a speed-time graph.

The Displacement is the Area Under a v-t Graph

1) The area under any section of a v-t graph is equal to the displacement (s) in that time interval.
2) For bits of the graph where the acceleration's constant, you can split the area into rectangles and triangles to work it out.
3) For a speed-time graph, the area under the graph is the distance travelled, rather than displacement.

You can find the area under a curved graph by counting the squares under the line and multiplying the number by the value of one square.

EXAMPLE: The velocity/time graph of a car's journey is plotted.
a) Calculate the acceleration of the car over the first 10 s.
b) How far does the car travel in the first 15 s of the journey?

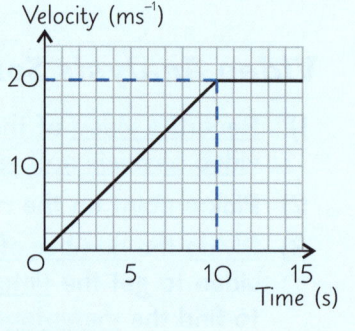

a) This is just the gradient of the line:
$a = (v - u) \div t$
$= (20 - 0) \div 10 = 2$ ms^{-2}

b) Split the area into a triangle and a rectangle, then add together their areas — remember the area of a triangle is ½ × base × height.

Area = (½ × 10 × 20) + (5 × 20)
= 200 m

Understanding motion graphs — it can be a real uphill struggle...

Remember — the acceleration of an object at a point on a v-t graph is the gradient of the curve at that point.

Q1 A car travels at a steady speed, then decelerates constantly to a stop. It is then stationary for a short time before accelerating with increasing acceleration. Sketch a velocity-time graph for the journey. [3 marks]

Section 1 — Dynamics

Forces

Force is a vector (p.13) — it has both a size and a direction. Arrows can represent forces acting on an object.

Forces Can be Contact or Non-Contact

1) A force is a push or a pull on an object that is caused by it interacting with something.
2) All forces are either contact or non-contact forces.
3) When two objects have to be touching for a force to act, that force is called a contact force, e.g. friction, air resistance, tension in ropes, reaction force, etc.
4) If the objects do not need to be touching for the force to act, the force is a non-contact force, e.g. magnetic force, gravitational force, electrostatic force, etc.
5) When two objects interact, there is a force produced on both objects. An interaction pair is a pair of forces that are equal and opposite and act on two interacting objects (p.21).

The Sun and the Earth are attracted to each other by the gravitational force. This is a non-contact force. An equal but opposite force of attraction is felt by both the Sun and the Earth.

Sun is attracted to the Earth

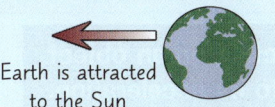
Earth is attracted to the Sun

A chair exerts a force on the ground, whilst the ground pushes back at the chair with the same force (the reaction force). Equal but opposite forces are felt by both the chair and the ground.

Chair pushes on ground
Ground pushes on chair

Free Body Force Diagrams Show All the Forces Acting on Objects

1) A free body force diagram shows an isolated body (an object or system on its own), and all the forces acting on it.
2) It should include every force acting on the body, but none of the forces it exerts on the rest of the world.
3) The sizes of the arrows show the relative magnitudes of the forces and the directions show the directions of the forces.

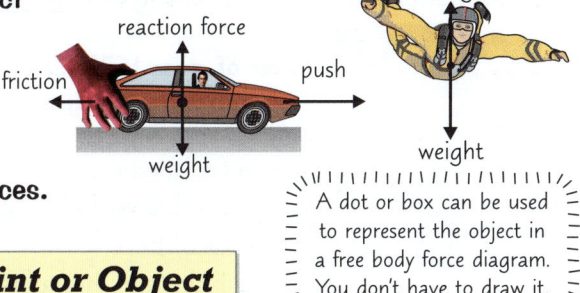

A dot or box can be used to represent the object in a free body force diagram. You don't have to draw it.

A Resultant Force is the Overall Force on a Point or Object

1) In most real situations there are at least two forces acting on an object along any direction.
2) If you have a number of forces acting at a single point, you can replace them with a resultant force with the same effect as all the original forces together.
3) You need to be able to calculate the resultant of two or more forces (see page 14 on resultant vectors).
4) Objects in equilibrium have a resultant force of zero — all of the forces are balanced.
5) A non-zero resultant force means the forces on an object are unbalanced. A non-zero resultant force is also called an unbalanced force.

- The reaction force felt by the van is equal to its weight. These forces act in opposite directions, so there is no resultant force in the vertical direction (1500 N − 1500 N = 0 N).
- The frictional force acting on the van is smaller than the driving force pushing it forward, so there is a resultant force in the horizontal direction.
- 1200 N − 1000 N = 200 N. So the resultant force is 200 N (to the left).

Consolidate all your forces into one easy-to-manage force...

Always sketch free body force diagrams for force questions. They mean you're less likely to forget any forces.

Q1 A car has a driving force of 2000 N and a weight of 1600 N. There is a total resistive force of 1200 N acting against the driving force. Draw the free body force diagram for the car. [2 marks]

Section 1 — Dynamics

Newton's First and Second Laws

Clever chap Isaac Newton — he came up with three handy laws about motion. This page covers the first two.

Newton's First Law — No Resultant Force Means No Change in Velocity

1) Newton's First Law says that:

   > An object will remain stationary or at a constant velocity unless acted upon by an external force.

2) If there is no resultant force on a stationary object, the object remains stationary — things don't just start moving on their own, there has to be a resultant force to get them started.
3) If there is no resultant force on a moving object it'll just carry on moving at the same velocity (at the same speed in the same direction) — for an object to travel with a uniform (constant) velocity, the driving forces and resistive forces (e.g. friction) must be balanced.
4) If there is an unbalanced force (non-zero resultant force) on an object, then the object will accelerate in the direction of the unbalanced force. This acceleration can take five different forms: starting, stopping, speeding up, slowing down and changing direction.

Newton's Second Law — An Unbalanced Force Causes an Acceleration

Newton's Second Law says:

> The unbalanced force acting on an object is directly proportional to its acceleration.

So any unbalanced force will produce an acceleration, and the formula for it is:

unbalanced force (N) = mass (kg) × acceleration (ms^{-2})   or $F = ma$

Remember that the F is always the unbalanced (resultant) force — that's pretty important.

EXAMPLE: A car of mass 1625 kg has an engine which provides a driving force of 5650 N. The drag force acting on the car is 450 N. Find its acceleration.

1) First draw a diagram showing the information given in the question. (there's no need to show the vertical forces).
2) Work out the unbalanced force.
3) State $F = ma$ and substitute in the values.
4) Rearrange to calculate acceleration.

Unbalanced force = 5650 − 450 = 5200 N
$F = ma$ so 5200 = 1625 × a
a = 5200 ÷ 1625 = 3.2 ms^{-2}

A Simple Experiment Demonstrates Newton's Second Law    PRACTICAL

1) The acceleration of a trolley on an air track can be used to investigate Newton's Second Law. (An air track is used as it greatly reduces the friction acting on the trolley.)
2) The force acting on the trolley is equal to the weight ($W = M \times g$, see page 22) of the hanging mass, M.
3) The hanging mass is released, pulling the trolley along the track.
4) By measuring the time and speed at which the trolley passes each light gate, its acceleration can be calculated (see p.17)
5) You can increase the force acting on the trolley by moving one of the masses from the trolley to the hanging mass and repeating the experiment.
6) If you plot your results on a graph of force against acceleration, you should get a straight line, showing that $F = ma$.

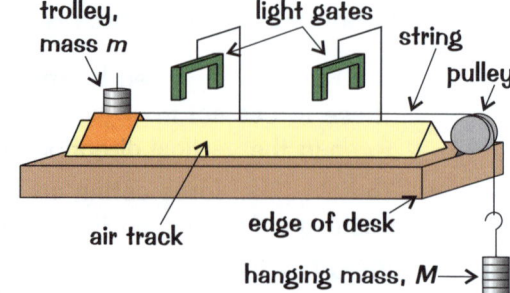

Air tracks and light gates — sounds like a band from the 80s...

Remember — Newton's First Law means an object at a steady speed doesn't need a resultant force to keep moving.

Q1   Calculate the unbalanced force acting on a 26 000 kg lorry with an acceleration of 1.5 ms^{-2}.   [3 marks]

Section 1 — Dynamics

Newton's Third Law

Another law eh? Isaac probably wasn't thinking about anyone having to revise them back in the 17th century.

Newton's Third Law: Equal and Opposite Forces Act on Interacting Objects

Newton's Third Law says: **If object A exerts a force on object B, then B exerts an equal but opposite force on A.**

1) Forces come in interaction pairs made up of an action force and a reaction force (sometimes called a 'Newton pair').
2) If you push something, say a shopping trolley, this is an action force. The trolley will push back against you, just as hard, this is the reaction force.
3) And as soon as you stop pushing, so does the trolley. Kinda clever really.
4) So far so good. The slightly tricky thing to get your head round is this — if the forces are always equal, how does anything ever go anywhere? The important thing to remember is that the two forces are acting on different objects.

a distraction force

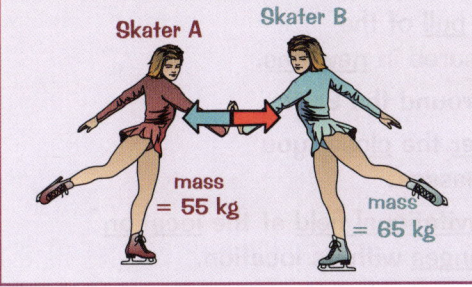

- When skater A pushes on skater B, she feels an equal and opposite force from skater B's hand (the 'reaction' force). Both skaters feel the same sized force, in opposite directions, and so accelerate away from each other.
- Skater A will be accelerated more than skater B, though, because she has a smaller mass — remember $a = F \div m$.

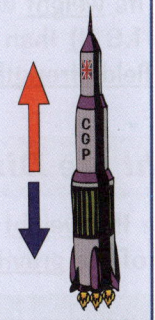

- When a rocket burns fuel it pushes hot gases out of the bottom of the rocket — the rocket exerts a backwards force on the gas.
- The hot gases exert an equal and opposite reaction force on the rocket.
- When this forwards force (thrust) is bigger than the weight of the rocket (or any other backwards forces), it will accelerate forwards.

There's more on Newton's Laws and space travel on p.35.

5) It's a bit more complicated for an object in equilibrium. Imagine a book sat on a table:

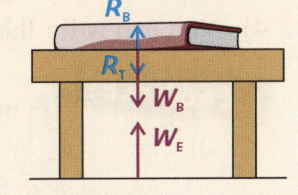

The weight of the book pulls it down, and the reaction force from the table pushes it up. This is NOT Newton's Third Law. These forces are different types and they're both acting on the book. The pairs of forces due to Newton's Third Law in this case are:
- The weight of book is pulled down by the force of gravity from Earth (W_B) and the book also pulls back up on the Earth (W_E).
- The reaction from the table is pushing up on the book (R_B) and the reaction force from the book is pushing down on the table (R_T).

Newton's fourth law — revision must be done with tea...

Newton's Third Law really trips people up, so make sure you understand exactly what the forces are acting on and how that results in movement (or lack of it). Then have a crack at this question to practise what you know.

Q1 a) State Newton's Third Law. [1 mark]
    b) Explain how a rocket uses fuel to propel itself forwards, with reference to Newton's Third Law. [3 marks]

Section 1 — Dynamics

Weight, Mass and Gravity

Now for something a bit more attractive — the force of gravity. Enjoy...

Gravitational Force is the Force of Attraction Between Masses

The force of gravity attracts all masses, but you only notice it when one of the masses is really really big, e.g. a planet. Anything near a planet or star is attracted to it very strongly. This has two important effects:

1) On the surface of a planet, it makes all things fall towards the ground.
2) It gives everything a weight.

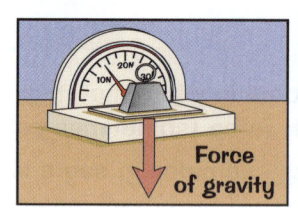

Weight and Mass are Not the Same

1) Mass is just the amount of 'stuff' in an object, it's not a force. For any given object this will have the same value anywhere in the universe.
2) Weight is the force acting on an object due to gravity (the pull of the gravitational force on the object). As it's a force, it's measured in newtons.
3) Close to Earth, weight is caused by the gravitational field around the Earth.
4) Gravitational field strength varies with location. It's stronger the closer you are to the mass causing the field, and stronger for larger masses.
5) The weight of an object depends on the strength of the gravitational field at the location of the object. This means that the weight of an object changes with its location.
6) For example, an object has the same mass whether it's on Earth or on the Moon — but its weight will be different. A 1 kg mass will weigh less on the Moon (about 1.6 N) than it does on Earth (about 9.8 N), simply because the gravitational field strength on the surface of the Moon is less.

Mass and Weight are Directly Proportional

1) You can calculate the weight of an object if you know its mass (m) and the strength of the gravitational field that it is in (g):

$$\text{weight (N)} = \text{mass (kg)} \times \text{gravitational field strength (Nkg}^{-1}\text{)}$$

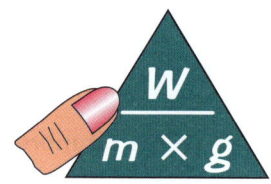

2) For Earth, $g = 9.8$ Nkg^{-1} and for the Moon it's around 1.6 Nkg^{-1}.
3) Increasing the mass of an object increases its weight. If you double the mass, the weight doubles too, so you can say that weight and mass are directly proportional.
4) You can write this, using the direct proportionality symbol, as $W \propto m$.

In the exam you'll be given values for the gravitational field strengths on different planets on the data sheet.

> **EXAMPLE:** A motorcycle weighs 2401 N on Earth. Calculate the mass of the motorcycle. ($g = 9.8$ Nkg^{-1})
> 1) First, state $W = mg$ and substitute in the numbers. $W = mg$ so $2401 = m \times 9.8$
> 2) Rearrange to find the mass. $m = 2401 \div 9.8 = 245$ kg

---

I don't think you understand the gravity of this situation...

Remember that weight is a force due to gravity. It changes depending on the strength of the gravitational field the object is in (and is directly proportional to the object's mass too). Mass won't change even if you're on Mars.

Q1   Calculate the weight in newtons of a 5 kg mass: a) on Earth ($g = 9.8$ Nkg^{-1})   [3 marks]
                                                                            b) on the Moon ($g = 1.6$ Nkg^{-1})   [2 marks]

Terminal Velocity

Ever wondered why it's so hard to run into a hurricane whilst wearing a sandwich board? Read on to find out...

Friction is Always There to Slow Things Down

1) If an object has no force propelling it along it will always slow down and stop because of friction (unless you're in space where there's nothing to rub against).
2) Friction always acts in the opposite direction to movement.
3) To travel at a steady speed, the driving force needs to balance the frictional forces (see page 20).
4) You get friction between two surfaces in contact, or when an object passes through a fluid (drag).

A fluid is a liquid or a gas.

Drag Increases as Speed Increases

1) Drag is the resistance you get in a fluid. Air resistance is a type of drag.
2) The most important factor by far in reducing drag is keeping the shape of the object streamlined. This is where the object is designed to allow fluid to flow easily across it, reducing drag. Parachutes work in the opposite way — they want as much drag as they can get.
3) Frictional forces from fluids always increase with speed. A car has much more friction to work against when travelling at 70 mph compared to 30 mph. So at 70 mph the engine has to work much harder just to maintain a steady speed.

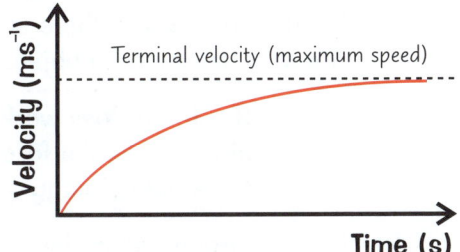
Air flows easily over a streamlined car.

Objects in Free-Fall in Fluids Reach a Terminal Velocity

When an object first begins falling, the force of gravity is much larger than the frictional force in the opposite direction, so it accelerates due to Newton's Second Law. As the speed increases the friction increases. This gradually reduces the acceleration. Eventually the frictional force is equal to the force of gravity, so the resultant force is zero. The object will have reached its maximum speed or terminal velocity and will fall at a steady speed due to Newton's First Law.

Terminal Velocity Depends on Shape and Area

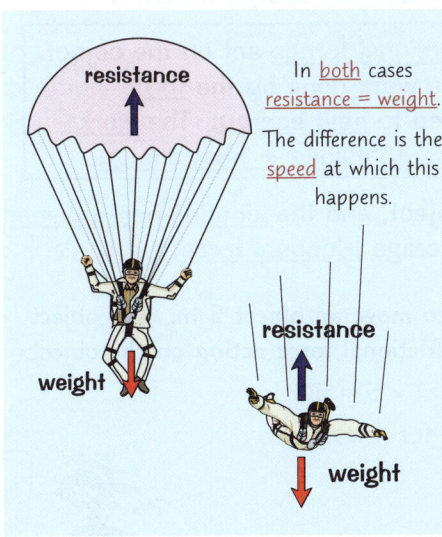

In both cases resistance = weight.

The difference is the speed at which this happens.

The accelerating force acting on all objects in free-fall is the force of gravity and it would make them all fall at the same rate if it wasn't for air resistance. This means that on the Moon, where there's no air, hamsters and feathers dropped simultaneously will hit the ground together. However, on Earth, air resistance causes things to fall at different speeds, and the terminal velocity of any object is determined by its air resistance in comparison to the force of gravity (its weight). The air resistance at a given speed depends on its shape and area.

The most important example is the human skydiver. Without his parachute open he has quite a small area and a force of "$W = mg$" pulling him down. He reaches a terminal velocity of about 54 ms^{-1}. But with the parachute open, there's much more air resistance (at any given speed) and still only the same force "$W = mg$" pulling him down. This means his terminal velocity comes down to about 7 ms^{-1}, which is a safe speed to hit the ground at.

Learning about air resistance — it can be a real drag...

Learn what terminal velocity is and why it happens, it's a term that crops up a fair bit in physics.

Q1   Explain why a ball falling from the top of a tall building reaches terminal velocity.   [3 marks]

Section 1 — Dynamics

Energy and Work Done

This page is all about work. No, not the kind you're already doing by reading this book...

Work is Done When a Force Moves an Object

When a FORCE makes an object MOVE, ENERGY IS TRANSFERRED and WORK IS DONE.

1) Whenever something begins to move, or changes how it's moving (e.g. speeds up, slows down or changes direction), something is providing some sort of effort (force) to move it.
2) The formula to calculate the amount of work done (energy transferred) when an object is moved through a distance by a force is:
3) Whether this energy is transferred usefully (e.g. by lifting a load) or wasted (e.g. dissipated to heat energy because of friction), you still say that 'work is done'. 'Work done' and 'energy transferred' are the same.

Energy is often said to have been converted between different types.

Work done (J)   Force (N)

$$W = F\,d$$

Distance moved in the direction of the force (m)

You might see E_w instead of W for work done. The units for work done can be joules or newton metres — these mean the same thing.

Energy is Always Conserved

1) The conservation of energy principle says that energy is always conserved:

Energy can be TRANSFERRED usefully, stored or dissipated, but can NEVER be CREATED or DESTROYED.

2) If in the process you're looking at, the energy before doesn't equal the energy after, you know that process can't happen.
3) If a process can happen, the formulas for work done (above) and the different types of energy (next page) can be used to calculate what will happen.
4) In situations where there are no frictional forces acting (i.e. no friction, no air resistance etc.), the work done on an object will be equal to the energy transferred usefully.

> If a force does work on an object and increases its velocity (in the same direction as the force), the object will gain kinetic energy. If there's no friction, the kinetic energy gained will equal the work done on the object by the force.

5) In most processes in the real world, some work must be done against resistive forces.
6) This causes some energy to be dissipated to heat energy (or thermal energy).
7) So the useful energy transferred won't equal the work done to cause the energy transfer.

> If work is done on an object to increase its velocity and frictional forces act on the object, the kinetic energy gained by the object will be less than the work done by the force applied to move the object. Some energy will be transferred to heat energy. The work done by the force to move the object equals the kinetic energy gained + heat energy.

8) If you know the work done by the force applied to move the object, and the kinetic energy gained, you can work out the work done by frictional forces and the average frictional force.

 A person applies a constant pushing force of 10 N to move an object 5 m. The object gains 40 J of kinetic energy. Calculate the average frictional force acting on the object.

1) Find the work done by the constant pushing force. $W = Fd = 10 \times 5 = 50$ J
2) The work done by friction is equal to the total work done minus the kinetic energy gained. $W = 50 - 40 = 10$ J
3) The average frictional force is the force causing the work done by friction. $W = Fd$
   $10 = F \times 5$
   So $F = 10 \div 5 = 2$ N

They said joule, Dave.

Energy transfers can be a lot of work...

Remember — work done is just energy transferred. That's why its units are joules. They're the same thing.

Q1   A force of 20 N pushes an object 20 cm. Calculate the work done on the object.   [4 marks]

Section 1 — Dynamics

Kinetic and Potential Energy

Time to look at two important types of energy — kinetic energy and gravitational potential energy.

A Moving Object has Kinetic Energy

1) Anything that is moving has kinetic energy (E_k). Energy is transferred to kinetic energy when an object speeds up and is transferred from kinetic energy when an object slows down.
2) The kinetic energy of an object depends on the object's mass and speed. The greater its mass and the faster it's going, the more kinetic energy it has.
3) There's a slightly tricky formula for it, so you have to concentrate a little bit harder for this one.

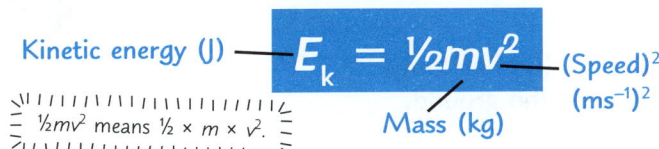

Kinetic energy (J) — $E_k = \tfrac{1}{2}mv^2$ — (Speed)² (ms⁻¹)²
Mass (kg)

½mv² means ½ × m × v².

EXAMPLE:
A car of mass 2500 kg is travelling at 20 ms⁻¹. Calculate the kinetic energy of the car.
$E_k = \tfrac{1}{2}mv^2 = \tfrac{1}{2} \times 2500 \times 20^2$
   $= 500\,000$ J

An Object at a Height has Gravitational Potential Energy

1) Lifting an object in a gravitational field requires work. This causes a transfer of energy to gravitational potential energy (E_p). The higher the object is lifted, the more E_p the object has.
2) The amount of E_p depends on the object's mass, its height and the strength of the gravitational field the object is in (p.22).
3) You can use this equation to find the change in E_p an object has for a change in height, h.

Gravitational potential energy (J) — $E_p = mgh$ — Height (m)
Mass (kg) Gravitational field strength (Nkg⁻¹)

Falling Objects Transfer Energy

1) When something falls, gravitational potential energy is transferred to kinetic energy.
2) For a falling object when there's no air resistance, conservation of energy (p.24) means: E_p lost = E_k gained

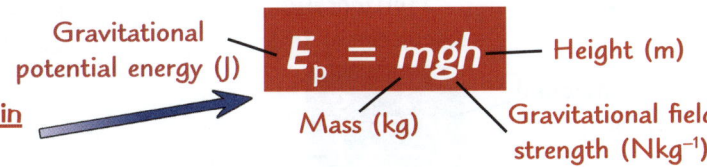

EXAMPLE:
A seagull is carrying a 0.20 kg sandwich. It is flying at a height of 4.0 m above the ground. It drops the sandwich. $g = 9.8$ Nkg⁻¹. You can ignore air resistance.
Calculate: a) the kinetic energy gained by the sandwich just before it hits the ground.
b) the speed of the sandwich just before it hits the ground.

a) Calculate the initial gravitational potential energy of the sandwich — this equals the final kinetic energy because E_p lost = E_k gained.
$E_p = mgh = 0.20 \times 9.8 \times 4.0$
     $= 7.84$ J of kinetic energy gained

b) State the equation for kinetic energy and substitute in the value you found for kinetic energy above. Rearrange to find the speed.
$E_k = \tfrac{1}{2}mv^2$
$7.84 = \tfrac{1}{2} \times 0.20 \times v^2$
so $v = \sqrt{\dfrac{2 \times 7.84}{0.20}} = 8.85 = 8.9$ ms⁻¹ (to 2 s.f.)

3) In real life, air resistance (p.23) acts against falling objects — it causes some energy to be transferred to other energy types, e.g. to heat energy and to the surroundings.
4) If you know the energy lost and the distance fallen, then you can use the formula $W = Fd$ to find the average frictional force, just like in the example on the previous page.

Make the most of your potential — jump on your bed...

Wow, that's a lot of energy equations. It's not over quite yet, now have a crack at this delightful question...

Q1   A 2.0 kg object is dropped from a height of 10.0 m. Calculate the kinetic energy of the object after it has fallen 5.0 m. Assume there is no air resistance ($g = 9.8$ Nkg⁻¹). [3 marks]

Section 1 — Dynamics

Projectile Motion

Calculators at the ready — it's time for some projectiles. It can be tricky at first, but you'll get the hang of it.

Projectile Motion Makes Curved Paths

1) A projectile is any object that is only acted on by the force of gravity.
2) This means that projectiles are always accelerating towards the ground (p.16).
3) Air resistance is always assumed to be negligible for projectiles — the only force is gravity.
4) A falling object is a projectile.
5) If a projectile is launched horizontally to give it an initial horizontal velocity then it will follow a curved path.
6) This is because it has a constant horizontal velocity, v_h, (no horizontal forces act) and a constant vertical acceleration towards the ground.

Horizontal and Vertical Motion are Independent of Each Other

When working with projectile motion questions, you can work out the horizontal and vertical motions separately. Luckily this makes things a lot easier, and gives you two nice equations to use:

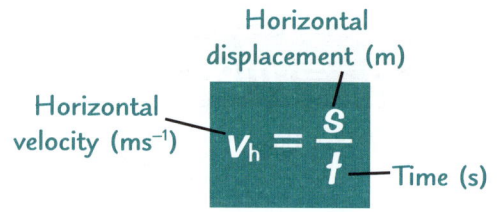

Horizontal velocity (ms⁻¹) $v_h = \dfrac{s}{t}$ — Horizontal displacement (m) — Time (s)

$v_v = u_v + at$

Final vertical velocity (ms⁻¹), Initial vertical velocity (ms⁻¹), Acceleration — usually g (ms⁻²), Time (s)

This equation has been rearranged from the acceleration equation on p.16.

EXAMPLE: Sharon fires a scale model of a TV talent show presenter horizontally with a velocity of 100 ms⁻¹ from a height above the ground. The vertical velocity just as the model hits the ground is 5.39 ms⁻¹. $g = 9.8$ ms⁻². Assume there is no air resistance

a) Calculate the time it takes for the object to reach the ground.
b) How far does the object travel horizontally before hitting the ground?

Think about what you already know:
1) It has constant acceleration under the force of gravity, $a = g = 9.8$ ms⁻².
2) You know $u_v = 0$ ms⁻¹ (the model is fired horizontally so there's no vertical velocity at first) and $v_v = 5.39$ ms⁻¹.
3) So state $v_v = u_v + at$ and rearrange to find the time.
4) You know that $v_h = 100$ ms⁻¹ so now that you know the time you can use $v_h = s \div t$ to find the horizontal displacement, s.

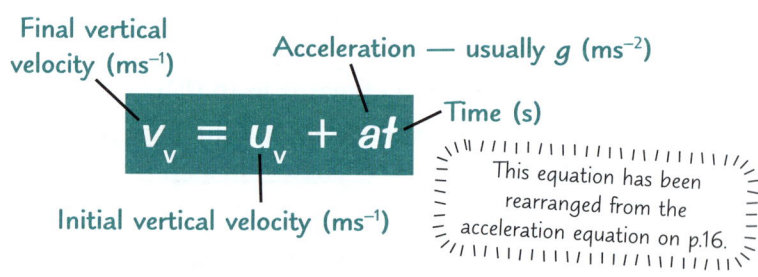

$v_v = u_v + at$ so $5.39 = 0 + (9.8 \times t)$

so $t = \dfrac{5.39 - 0}{9.8} = 0.55$ s

$v_h = s \div t$

$100 = s \div 0.55$ so $s = 100 \times 0.55 = 55$ m

This page is giving me projectile motion sickness...

It helps to draw a diagram when answering projectile motion questions. Label the diagram with any horizontal and vertical velocities, accelerations, times and distances that you've been given in the question.

Q1 A ball is thrown horizontally with a velocity of 10 ms⁻¹. It hits the ground after 4 s. Calculate the horizontal distance the ball travelled before hitting the ground. Assume there is no air resistance. **[3 marks]**

Section 1 — Dynamics

More Projectile Motion and Satellites

And there's even more on projectile motion... when does it end... soon is the answer.

You can Draw Horizontal and Vertical Velocity-Time Graphs for Projectiles

1) Unfortunately you need to know two different velocity-time (v-t) graphs for a projectile — one for vertical velocity (v_v) and one for horizontal velocity (v_h).
2) A v_h-t graph for a projectile launched horizontally is a straight horizontal line because horizontal velocity is constant.
3) A v_v-t graph for a projectile launched horizontally is a straight uphill line because there is a constant acceleration of g.

Remember, air resistance is negligible for projectile motion. The force of gravity is the only force so the horizontal velocity and vertical acceleration are constant.

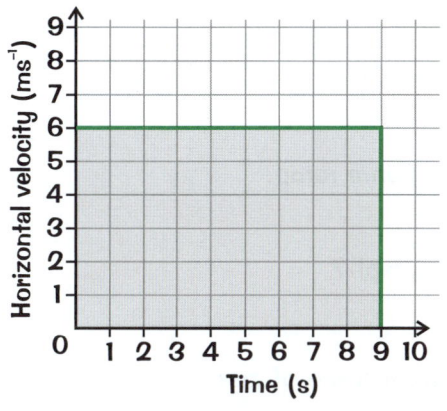
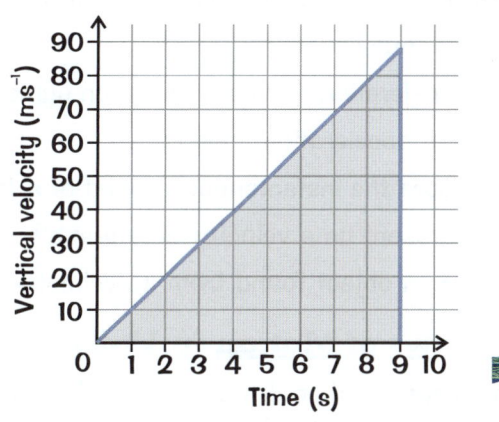
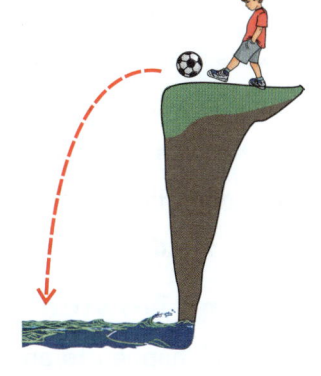

4) The area underneath a v_h-t graph gives the range or horizontal distance travelled.
5) The area under a v_v-t graph gives the height or vertical distance travelled.

Satellites Move with Projectile Motion

1) A satellite is a type of projectile. It's launched horizontally and the only force acting on it is its weight due to gravity. Space is a vacuum so there is no air resistance to act on it.
2) It accelerates towards Earth in free-fall and has a constant horizontal velocity.
3) Launching a projectile usually results in it crashing down to the ground, which wouldn't be great for a satellite.
4) Launching a projectile with a faster horizontal speed increases the horizontal distance covered before hitting the Earth ($s = v_h \times t$, p.26).
5) The Earth's surface is curved, so if you launch a satellite fast enough then its curved path will match the curvature of the Earth.
6) When this happens the satellite will be in free-fall towards the Earth forever without reaching it. This is known as orbiting.
7) If a satellite is launched too fast, its path won't curve enough and it will fly off into space.
8) The horizontal velocity has to be large enough to make sure it doesn't get closer to the Earth. The weight needs to be large enough that the satellite doesn't get further away from Earth.

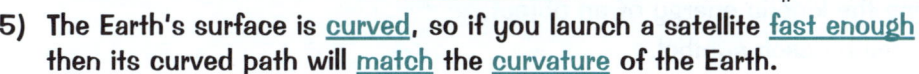
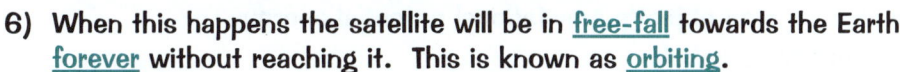

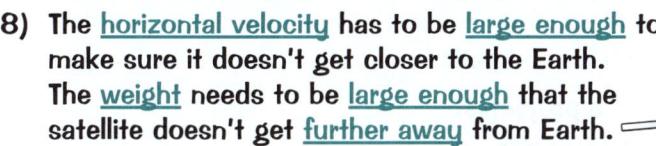
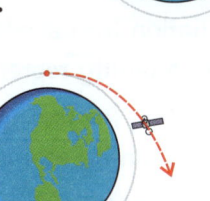
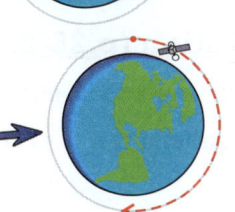

Revise with a constant velocity and don't slow down...

Remember that good ol' fairy tale of Goldilocks the satellite. The velocity wasn't too fast or too slow, but just right.

Q1   A cricket player throws a cricket ball horizontally at a constant velocity. Draw a graph of the vertical velocity against time for the ball after it leaves the player's hand. You can ignore air resistance.   [2 marks]

Section 1 — Dynamics

Revision Questions for Section 1

Well, that wraps up Section 1 — go back over any pages you don't feel 100% about, then try these questions.
- Try these questions and tick off each one when you get it right.
- When you've done all the questions for a topic and are completely happy with it, tick off the topic.

Distance, Speed and Acceleration (p.13-18)

1) Give two examples of scalar quantities and two examples of vector quantities.
2) How do you find the resultant of two vectors which are acting in opposite directions to each other?
3) Describe two ways that you can find the resultant of two vectors at right angles to each other.
4) State the equation that can be used to find displacement from velocity and time.
5) What is meant by 'instantaneous speed'?
6) What is the equation for acceleration? What does each symbol mean?
7) What does the term 'uniform acceleration' mean?
8) Describe a method to measure the instantaneous speed of a trolley on a ramp.
9) What does the gradient represent on a velocity-time graph?
10) How is the displacement of an object found from its velocity-time graph?

Forces and Newton's Laws of Motion (p.19-23)

11) What will happen to an object's motion if it is acted on by a resultant force of zero?
12) What will happen to an object's motion if it is acted on by a non-zero resultant force?
13) Give the equation for Newton's Second Law, including the units for each quantity.
14) Give an example of Newton's Third Law in action.
15) What is the difference between weight and mass?
16) What is the formula for calculating the weight of an object?
17) Use Newton's Laws to explain how an object in free-fall reaches its terminal velocity.

Energy (p.24-25)

18) Give the equation for work done by a force moving an object through a distance, including the units.
19) State the conservation of energy principle.
20) If energy is transferred to the kinetic energy of an object, what happens to the object's speed?
21) Give the equation for calculating the kinetic energy of an object, including the quantity represented by each symbol.
22) Give the equation for finding the change in an object's gravitational potential energy, including the quantity represented by each symbol.
23) What type of energy is gravitational potential energy transferred to by an object in free-fall?

Projectile Motion (p.26-27)

24) Explain why a projectile launched horizontally follows a curved path.
25) State the equations for: a) the horizontal velocity of a projectile,
                                b) the vertical velocity of a projectile.
26) Explain why a satellite is a type of projectile.
27) Explain how a satellite's motion depends on its horizontal velocity.

Section 2 — Space

Our Solar System, Our Galaxy and the Universe

There are billions of galaxies in the universe, and each and every galaxy contains loads of stars and planets...

We are Part of the Milky Way Galaxy

1) The universe is a large collection of billions of galaxies.
2) A galaxy is a large collection of stars. A star is hot, dense, luminous sphere of gas.
3) Our Sun is just one of many billions of stars which form the Milky Way galaxy. Our Sun is about halfway along one of the spiral arms of the Milky Way.
4) The distance between neighbouring stars in the galaxy is often millions of times greater than the distance between planets in our solar system.
5) The force which keeps the stars together in a galaxy is the force of gravity. And like most things in the universe, galaxies rotate — a bit like a Catherine wheel.
6) Galaxies themselves are often millions of times further apart than the stars are within a galaxy.
7) So the universe is mostly empty space and is really, really BIG.

You are here.

Our Solar System has One Star — The Sun

The Solar System is all the stuff that orbits the Sun (or orbits something that orbits the Sun). It includes:

1) Planets — these are large objects that orbit a star. The eight planets in the Solar System are, in order (from the Sun outwards): Mercury, Venus, Earth, Mars, Jupiter, Saturn, Uranus and Neptune. A planet outside of the Solar System is called an exoplanet.
2) Dwarf planets, like our pal Pluto. These are planet-like objects that aren't big enough to be planets.
3) Moons — these orbit planets with almost circular orbits. They're a type of natural satellite (i.e. they're not man-made).
4) Artificial satellites (ones humans have built) that usually orbit the Earth in fairly circular orbits.
5) Asteroids — lumps of rock and metal that orbit the Sun. They're usually found in the asteroid belt.

A satellite is an object that orbits a second, more massive object.

Distances in Space are Measured in Light Years

1) All electromagnetic waves travel at the speed of light (p.61) in a vacuum. This speed is about 3.00×10^8 ms^{-1}.
2) The distance that electromagnetic waves travel through a vacuum in one year is called a light year. 1 light year is equal to about 9.5×10^{15} m.
3) So if a star is 5 light years away from Earth, is takes 5 years for light from the star to reach Earth.
4) To convert between light years and metres, first find out how long it takes the light to travel the distance in seconds.
5) Then plug this time into $d = vt$ (p.15) where v is the speed of light.

EXAMPLE: The Andromeda galaxy is the closest galaxy to the Milky Way. It is 2.5×10^6 light years away. Calculate this distance in metres.

1) Find out how long, in seconds, it takes for the light to travel the distance given — the number of seconds in one year is 60 seconds × 60 minutes × 24 hours × 365.25 days.

    $2.5 \times 10^6 \times 60 \times 60 \times 24 \times 365.25$
    $= 7.8894 \times 10^{13}$ s

2) Substitute this into $d = vt$.

    $d = vt = (3 \times 10^8) \times (7.8894 \times 10^{13})$
    $= 2.366... \times 10^{22} = 2.4 \times 10^{22}$ m (to 2 s.f.)

Revision's hard work — you've got to plan et...

Make sure you can tell a moon from a planet, and a galaxy from the Solar System. Then have a go at these.

Q1 Give the name of the galaxy that the Solar System is located in. [1 mark]

Q2 The nearest star to our Sun is 4.2 light years away. Calculate this distance in metres. [3 marks]

Origin of the Universe

'How did the universe begin?' is a tricky question that we just can't answer. Our best guess is the Big Bang.

The Big Bang — the Universe Started with an Explosion

1) Right now, all the galaxies are moving away from each other at great speed.
2) This observation is explained by the Big Bang theory — which is the currently accepted theory for how the universe began.
3) The theory says that initially, all the matter in the universe occupied a very small space.
4) This tiny space was very dense and very hot.
5) Then it 'exploded' — space started expanding, and it is this expansion that's still going on.
6) The Big Bang theory gives a finite age for the universe of around 14 billion years.

Telescopes and Satellites are used to Observe the Universe

1) Our knowledge and understanding of the universe has come from observations made using telescopes and satellites.
2) Different astronomical objects produce different wavelengths of EM radiation (p.61), so we need a range of telescopes that can observe the whole of the electromagnetic spectrum.

Radio Telescopes on Earth Receive Radio Signals From Outer Space

1) In 1964, a very sensitive radio telescope discovered the cosmic microwave background (CMB).
2) The CMB is electromagnetic radiation (p.61) left behind from the beginning of the universe. It provides a massive piece of evidence in support of the Big Bang theory.
3) The CMB was discovered using a telescope on Earth. However, the problem with using telescopes on Earth is that a lot of electromagnetic radiation from space is absorbed by the Earth's atmosphere.
4) Sending satellites and telescopes out into space can give more accurate measurements.

COBE Looked for Cosmic Microwave Background Radiation

1) COBE was a satellite in space from 1989 to 1993, it stands for Cosmic Background Explorer.
2) COBE was used to investigate the cosmic microwave background radiation.
3) Measurements taken by COBE supported the Big Bang theory and helped astronomers to understand the universe's history.

SETI Looks for Radio Signals from Other Planets

1) SETI stands for Search for ExtraTerrestrial Intelligence. Scientists on various SETI projects are looking for radio waves coming to Earth from outer space.
2) Radio signals from space could be a sign of intelligent life. Us Earthlings are constantly beaming radio, TV and radar into space for any passing aliens to detect, so if intelligent life exists somewhere in the universe, they might have built transmitters to send out signals like ours.
3) Most of the radio signals from outer space come from giant stars and other astronomical objects — SETI is looking for a meaningful signal amongst the 'noise'.
4) SETI has been going for about 60 years but it's not found anything.

In the beginning, there were — no exams...

The Big Bang theory is the best one we've got to explain how the universe began, but it may need some tweaking in the future if we find new evidence it can't explain. Scientists, pfft, don't they ever finish anything?

Q1   Approximately how old is the universe? [1 mark]

Section 2 — Space

Observing the Universe

The light from stars doesn't just make the sky look pretty — it can actually tell you what stars are made of...

Continuous Spectra Contain All Possible Frequencies a Star Emits

1) All hot objects like stars emit radiation. Hot objects emit a continuous range of frequencies — a continuous spectrum (it doesn't have any gaps).
2) The light of a continuous spectrum can be observed by passing the light through a prism.
3) The prism refracts (p.61) each frequency by a different amount, so the continuous spectrum is split.

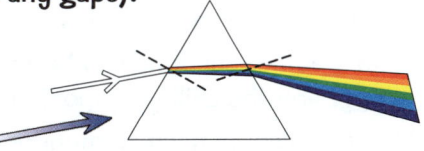

Emission Spectra — Certain Frequencies are Emitted by an Element

1) When an element is heated, it emits radiation of certain frequencies due to changes in the atom.
2) When an element emits radiation, the spectrum coming from it will show a line for each particular frequency emitted. The lines are called emission lines, and the spectrum is called an emission spectrum.
3) Each element can only emit certain frequencies of radiation, so each element has its own unique emission spectrum.

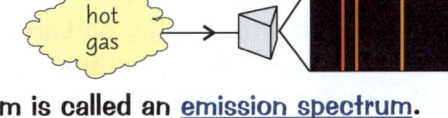 

Emission line

Absorption Spectra — Certain Frequencies are Absorbed by Elements

1) If a continuous spectrum of radiation passes through a gas, certain frequencies are absorbed.
2) When a certain frequency is absorbed, this particular frequency of light is shown by a gap in the continuous spectrum. The gap is called an absorption line and the spectrum is an absorption spectrum.
3) Each different element absorbs different frequencies of radiation, depending on its atomic structure.
4) So each element has its own unique absorption lines.
5) The absorption spectrum of an element matches its emission spectrum.

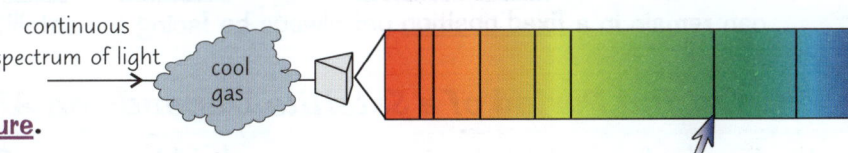

Absorption line

Astronomers Use Spectra to Work Out What Stars are Made Of

1) A star emits a continuous spectrum of radiation.
2) This radiation passes through the gases in the star's atmosphere, which results in an absorption line spectrum.
3) By looking at the position of the lines in the star's spectrum, you can work out what chemical elements are present in the star's atmosphere — by comparing it with known emission or absorption spectra in the lab.

Stellar spectrum containing H, He and Na
Hydrogen, H
Helium, He
Sodium, Na

What do you call a star detective? In-Spectra...

You could be asked to work out the elements in a star in the exam — have a go at this question to see if you get it.

Q1   The diagram on the right shows the absorption spectrum for a star, and the absorption spectra for three elements, A, B and C. Use the diagram to determine which elements are present in the star. [2 marks]

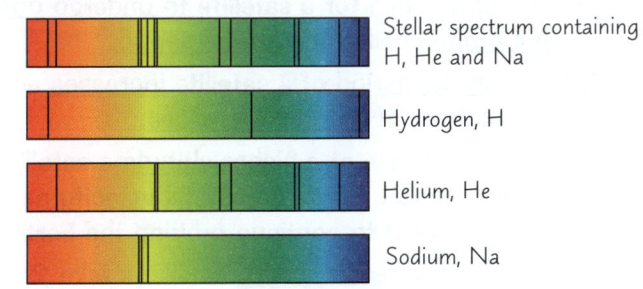

Section 2 — Space

Satellites

A satellite is any object that orbits around a larger object in space. There are natural satellites, like moons, but this page just looks at the artificial ones that we put there ourselves — used for GPS, satellite phones etc...

Satellites Have Loads of Uses

1) Satellites are used for GPS — the Global Positioning System. GPS satellites are used for navigation, e.g. in cars or on mobile phones.
2) Images of weather systems can be taken by satellites. This allows accurate weather forecasting, and the ability to monitor dangerous weather systems like hurricanes.
3) Satellites can also be used to monitor climate change and pollution levels.
4) Satellites, like the International Space Station and the Hubble telescope, are often used for scientific purposes and space exploration instead of telescopes on the ground. This is because the atmosphere can interfere with signals coming from outer space.
5) Communication to and from satellites (including for satellite TV and phones) uses microwaves (p.62) that can pass easily through the atmosphere.
6) For satellite TV, the signal from a transmitter on Earth is transmitted into space where it's absorbed by the satellite receiver dish orbiting the Earth. The satellite transmits the signal back to Earth in a different direction where it's received by a satellite dish on the ground.

Geostationary Satellites Stay Over the Same Point on Earth

1) Geostationary satellites orbit at about 36 000 km above Earth's equator and orbit once every 24 hours.
2) This means that they stay above the same point on the Earth's surface because the Earth rotates with them.
3) This is useful for communications because antennas on Earth can remain in a fixed position yet always be facing the satellite.

The Orbital Period of a Satellite Depends on Altitude

1) In order for a satellite to stay at the same height above the Earth, its horizontal velocity and weight need to be just right (p.27).
2) The horizontal velocity needs to be large enough so that it doesn't move closer to Earth, and its weight needs to be large enough so that it doesn't move away from Earth.
3) The time taken for a satellite to undergo one full orbit is called the orbital period.
4) The orbital period of a satellite increases as the altitude of its orbit increases.
5) This is because at a higher altitude a satellite has a lower weight (p.22), so its horizontal velocity needs to decrease in order for it to continue orbiting the Earth.
6) This is why geostationary satellites take 24 hours to orbit the Earth, but lower orbiting satellites, like weather satellites, can orbit the Earth in less than 2 hours.
7) The mass of a satellite orbiting at a particular altitude doesn't affect its period — if two satellites with different masses are orbiting at the same altitude, they will have the same orbital period.

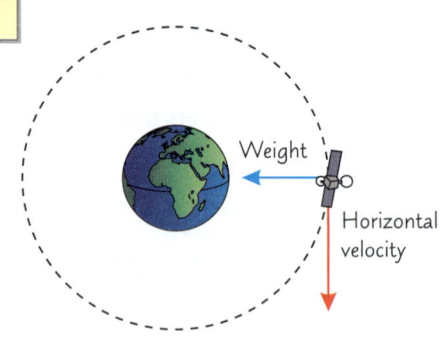

When in orbit, a satellite is in constant free-fall (see p.27). This is why astronauts orbiting the Earth (e.g. on the ISS) experience 'weightlessness' — they do still have a weight, they are just free-falling.

So you can thank satellites next time you ring home from Everest...

Don't forget the link between a satellite's altitude and its orbital period. It's a common exam question.

Q1 A satellite is orbiting the Earth at an altitude of 405 km. The satellite reduces its orbit to 390 km. What will happen to the orbital period of the satellite when it lowers its altitude? [1 mark]

Challenges and Risks of Space Travel

Now it's time for the fun part — space travel. There's a load of information to take in over these next few pages, so take your time and be sure to re-read them a few times.

There are Risks to Astronauts During Space Travel

1) The risks to astronauts begin straight away when the space rocket is taking off because very large amounts of fuel have to be carried. The fuel is highly flammable and a fault could cause an explosion.

2) The Earth's atmosphere protects you from harmful ionising radiation called cosmic rays (p.70) — these come from space and the Sun. In space, astronauts receive a much higher dose of ionising radiation, which can damage cells in the body, p.70. Scientists are working on shielding for spacecraft to protect astronauts from cosmic rays.

3) There are lots of complex life support systems on spacecraft and in spacesuits — if any of these go wrong, the astronauts could be in a lot of danger:

   - Earth's atmosphere contains oxygen but space doesn't. The spacecraft and space suits have an oxygen supply, but astronauts could be without oxygen if something goes wrong.
   - Our atmosphere keeps Earth at a pretty constant temperature — the temperature change between day and night isn't massive. However, in space the temperature changes by huge amounts. For example, the outside of the International Space Station reaches a temperature of 120 °C when it's in sunlight, and gets as low as −160 °C when it's in the dark. So spacecraft need advanced temperature control systems to keep the astronauts safe.
   - Space is a vacuum — the pressure in space is almost zero. There is a very large pressure differential between space and a human body. Spacecraft and spacesuits have to be pressurised so that the astronauts are at the same pressure as they would be on Earth. If these weren't pressurised, the pressure difference would cause all the liquid in your body to boil — ouch.

Spacecraft Need to Produce Electricity

1) All spacecraft need a constant supply of electricity in order to run the electrical equipment on board.

2) On a manned spacecraft the life support systems required to regulate temperature and pressure and to supply oxygen and water need even more electricity.

3) Photovoltaic (solar) cells (p.41) are a possible way of powering the life support systems needed for manned space missions. Photovoltaic cells convert light energy from the Sun to electrical energy.

4) If photovoltaic cells were used on a spacecraft travelling towards the Sun, there would need to be a way to turn the cells away from the Sun to prevent them overheating. Whereas, a spacecraft travelling away from the Sun may need to increase the area of its photovoltaic cells in order to harness enough energy. This would present problems since leaving Earth with giant solar cell arrays would be tricky due to the increased drag.

5) An example of a spacecraft powered by photovoltaic cells is the International Space Station (ISS). These arrays can be rotated so that they absorb maximum sunlight.

6) The ISS spends part of its orbit is in the Earth's shadow. During this time it can't use its solar cells to produce electricity. Instead it relies on a backup battery which is charged during sunlight hours.

The ISS orbits the Earth roughly 220 miles above the Earth's surface — it's a habitable satellite.

Space crafts — an origami club for astronauts.

This page has a links to other sections, like cosmic rays in radiation, and photovoltaic cells in electricity. The exam questions might link these sections together, so you need to be confident on them all.

Q1 Explain why astronauts are more at risk from cancer than people on Earth. [2 marks]

More Challenges and Risks of Space Travel

As if there weren't enough space travel challenges and risks on the previous page, here's a whole other page...

Spacecraft Travel Long Distances

Space journeys cover extremely long distances, so spacecraft need to travel at high speeds to cover these distances in a reasonable length of time. Carrying enough fuel for this can be a real challenge.

Ion Drives use Small Amounts of Fuel

1) Ion drives are more efficient than regular thrusters — they use less fuel and reach higher top speeds.
2) Ion drives ionise propellant by adding or removing electrons to produce ions. The ions are accelerated to produce thrust.
3) Ion drives use a small amount of fuel to give a small unbalanced force (p.20) over a long time.
4) This reduces costs because the spacecraft can be smaller — less fuel needs to be carried on board.

Planets, Moons and Asteroids can be used for Catapults

1) Fast moving planets, moons, or asteroids can be used for gravitational catapults (sometimes called slingshots) to accelerate or change the direction of a spacecraft.
2) When the spacecraft enters the gravitational field of the planet (or moon or asteroid) it is accelerated towards the planet.
3) The spacecraft then leaves the planet's gravitational field at a higher speed — some of the planet's kinetic energy has been transferred to the spacecraft.
4) This allows the spacecraft to travel a huge distance using hardly any fuel.

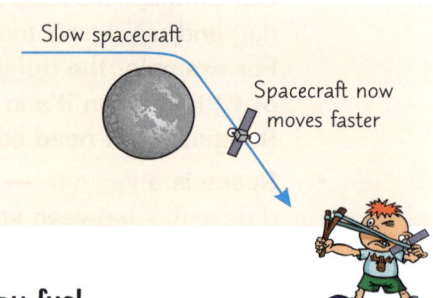

Precise Manoeuvres are Tricky in Space due to Zero Friction

1) Spacecraft often have to do very precise manoeuvres, like entering the Earth's atmosphere at an exact angle, or docking with another spacecraft like the ISS.
2) This is difficult as space is a zero friction environment, so friction doesn't slow down the spacecraft. Thrusters on each side of the spacecraft need to carefully fire very small amounts of fuel to align the spacecraft correctly.

A Spacecraft Gets Extremely Hot During Re-Entry

1) Spacecraft and astronauts have to survive re-entering the Earth's atmosphere.
2) The particles in the Earth's atmosphere produce a very big frictional force on the surface of the spacecraft as it travels through the atmosphere at high speeds.
3) The frictional force does work (p.24) on the spacecraft, converting some of the spacecraft's kinetic energy to heat energy. This can heat the spacecraft up to temperatures as high as 1600 °C.
4) Ablation heat shields are used to protect the spacecraft. These are shields with protective layers of material on the spacecraft that burn up on re-entry to dissipate heat energy to the surroundings, preventing the spacecraft from becoming too hot.
5) Heat energy is absorbed by the shield, increasing its temperature.
6) The heat energy absorbed can also cause some of the protective layers to turn into a gas.
7) The amount of heat energy absorbed by the heat shield heating up depends on the specific heat capacity, p.51. The amount of energy absorbed when layers of the shield are turning into a gas depends on the specific latent heat of vaporisation, p.52.

Warning — high risk of revision headache...

That's all of the risk and challenges you need to know. Now cover them up and see what you've remembered.

Q1 Vast distances are involved in space travel. Explain one way that this challenge is overcome. [2 marks]

Section 2 — Space

Mechanics of Space Travel

Newton's Second and Third Laws come in really handy when understanding how rockets move...

Weight is Different on Different Planets

1) The mass of an object doesn't change, it's just a measure of how much matter something contains.
2) However the weight of an object is a measure of the force of gravity on an object. This means that weight is affected by gravitational field strength, g. See p.22 for more on mass and weight.
3) $W = mg$, so on planets with a higher gravitational field strength, an object's weight is bigger.
4) The further away you get from a planet (or moon), the weaker the gravitational field strength is, so the weight of an object decreases.
5) Once you are far enough away from a planet, the gravitational field strength equals zero, and an object becomes weightless.

The gravitational field strengths on the surfaces of different planets are given on the data sheet in the exam.

Newton's Second Law can Describe a Rocket Taking Off

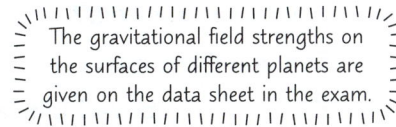

1) Newton's Second Law relates mass, acceleration and the unbalanced force acting on an object — $F = ma$ (see page 20).
2) In order for a rocket to lift off, it needs to accelerate from rest. So due to Newton's Second Law, there needs to be a forwards unbalanced force — the forwards force (thrust) needs to be bigger than the backwards force (weight).
3) If this is the case, the rocket's velocity will start to increase.
4) When the rocket begins to move, air resistance will start to act in the opposite direction to its motion. Air resistance will increase as the rocket's velocity increases.
5) The thrust now has to be greater than both the weight and the air resistance to continue accelerating.
6) As the rocket gets further from the Earth:
   - The atmosphere becomes thinner so air resistance decreases.
   - The gravitational field of the Earth becomes weaker and fuel is burnt so the rocket's weight decreases.
7) The rocket's thrust will be altered to make sure that the rocket continues to move forwards until it escapes Earth's atmosphere.
8) For a spacecraft to land safely, it needs to descend slowly. For this to happen, the thrust needs to be bigger than and in the opposite direction to the force of gravity. This means that there is a negative acceleration (deceleration) and the spacecraft slows down as it reaches the surface.
9) Parachutes can be used to slow down a spacecraft for landing. Parachutes increase air resistance so that the spacecraft decelerates, see page 23.

Newton's Third Law can Explain Rocket Propulsion

1) Newton's Third Law says that every 'action' force has an equal 'reaction' force that acts in the opposite direction. This explains how rockets move in space when there is no friction:

   - When a rocket burns fuel it pushes hot gases out of the bottom of the rocket. The rocket exerts a backward force on the gas — this is the action force.
   - The hot gases exert an equal and opposite forward force on the rocket — this is the reaction force.

   You've met this already on p.21

2) There is no air resistance in space, and far enough away from a planet there is no weight, so the reaction force is an unbalanced force on the rocket. The rocket will accelerate forwards as $F = ma$.

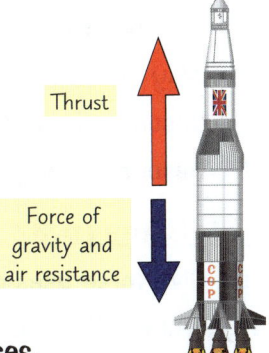

I have a reaction to forces — they bring me out in a rash...

There's loads more about Newton's Laws back in Section 1, so nip back to pages 20-21 if you need a reminder.

Q1   Explain using Newton's Third Law how a rocket uses thrusters to propel itself forwards.   [2 marks]

Section 2 — Space

Revision Questions for Section 2

That's Section 2 all wrapped up — time to put yourself to the test and find out how much you really know.
- Try these questions and tick off each one when you get it right.
- When you've done all the questions for a topic and are completely happy with it, tick off the topic.

Cosmology (p.29-31) ☐

1) What is a galaxy?
2) Give an example of a natural satellite and an artificial one.
3) What is an asteroid?
4) Define a light year.
5) How do you convert between light years and metres?
6) Name and describe the current theory of how the universe began.
7) True or false? The universe is still expanding.
8) Why do we need to use telescopes that observe a range of wavelengths of EM radiation?
9) Describe the difference between a continuous spectrum and an absorption line spectrum.
10) Describe how you can use a line spectrum to work out what elements a star is made from.

Satellites (p.32) ☐

11) Give three uses of satellites.
12) What is the approximate altitude of a geostationary satellite?
13) What is the period of a geostationary satellite?
14) State what would happen to the period of a satellite if its altitude was increased.

Space Travel (p.33-35) ☐

15) Why does the fuel carried on board a spacecraft present a danger to the astronauts?
16) How can a spacecraft generate electricity?
17) How can the gravitational field of a planet be used to accelerate a spacecraft?
18) Why do spacecraft heat up when they re-enter Earth's atmosphere?
19) How can a spacecraft be protected from heat when re-entering the Earth's atmosphere?
20) Explain how the unbalanced forces on a rocket change as it takes off.
21) What direction does a rocket's thrust need to act in order to slow down the rocket as it approaches a planet's surface?

Section 3 — Electricity

Charge and Electric Fields

Electric fields — much less green and much more shocking than the fields you're used to.

Electric Charges Create an Electric Field

1) An electric field is created around any electrically charged object.
2) The closer to the object you get, the stronger the field is.

Charged Objects in an Electric Field feel a Force

1) When a charged object is placed in the electric field of another object, it feels a force.
2) This force causes attraction or repulsion. Like charges repel and opposite charges attract (see below).
3) The force is caused by the electric fields of each charged object interacting with each other.
4) The force on an object is linked to the strength of the electric field it is in.
5) As you increase the distance between the charged objects, the force between them gets smaller.

Field Lines Show the Path of a Charged Particle

1) You can show an electric field around an object using field lines.
2) Electric field lines go from positive to negative and they're always at a right angle to the surface of the charged object.
3) The closer together the lines are, the stronger the field is. The further from a charge you go, the further apart the lines are and so the weaker the field is.
4) The field lines show the direction that a force would act on a positive charge placed at each point. A negative charge would feel an opposite force.
5) Field lines can be used to work out the path that a positive or negative charge would take if placed in the field.
6) You need to know what the following fields look like:

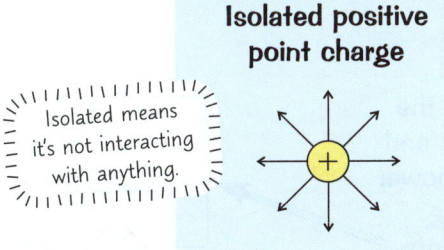

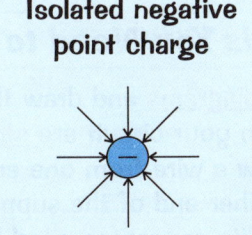

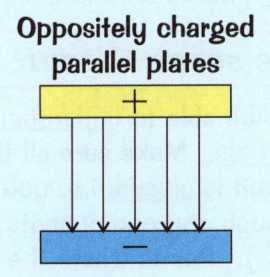

Isolated means it's not interacting with anything.

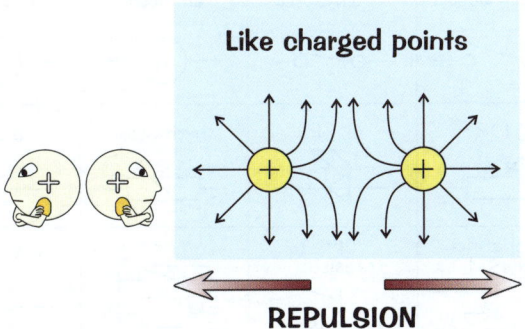

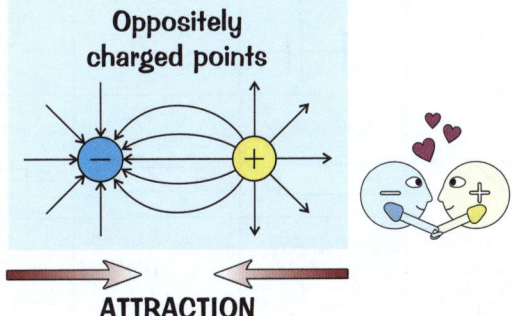

Electric felines — lines between charged cats...

Remember field lines show the path that a positive charge takes — they always go from positive to negative.

Q1 State which direction a negatively charged particle would move if placed near a positive point charge.
[1 mark]

Electrical Current and Circuit Symbols

It's pretty bad news if the word current makes you think of delicious cakes instead of physics...

Current is the Flow of Electrical Charge

1) Electrical current is the electrical charge transferred per unit time.
2) Electric current needs a source of potential difference to flow (p.39).
3) The unit of current is the ampere, A.
4) In metals the electrical charge carriers are electrons.
5) We normally say that current in a circuit flows from positive (+ve) to negative (−ve). Alas, electrons were discovered long after that was decided and they turned out to be negatively charged — unlucky. This means they actually flow from −ve to +ve, opposite to the flow of "conventional current".
6) In a single, closed loop (like the one above) the current has the same value everywhere in the circuit (see p.43).

Some Materials Carry Charge Better than Others

1) Electrical charge travels easily through electrical conductors, like metals.
2) Materials that do not let electrical charge pass through them easily are called electrical insulators. Plastic, wood, glass and rubber are good electrical insulators.

Total Charge Through a Circuit Depends on Current and Time

When current flows past a point in a circuit for a length of time then the charge that has passed is given by this formula:

Charge (coulombs, C) — $Q = It$ — Current (A), Time (s)

EXAMPLE:
A battery charger passes a current of 2.0 A through a cell over a period of 2.5 hours. How much charge is transferred to the cell?
$Q = It = 2.0 \times (2.5 \times 60 \times 60)$
$= 18\,000$ C

More charge passes around the circuit when a larger current flows.

There are some Circuit Symbols You Need to Know

You need to be able to understand circuit diagrams and draw them using the correct symbols. Make sure all the wires in your circuit are straight lines and that the circuit is closed, i.e. you can follow a wire from one end of the power supply, through any components, to the other end of the supply (ignoring any switches). Points where the circuit splits are represented by black dots.

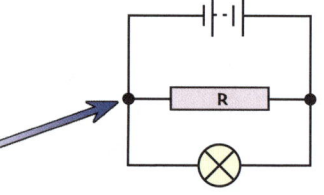

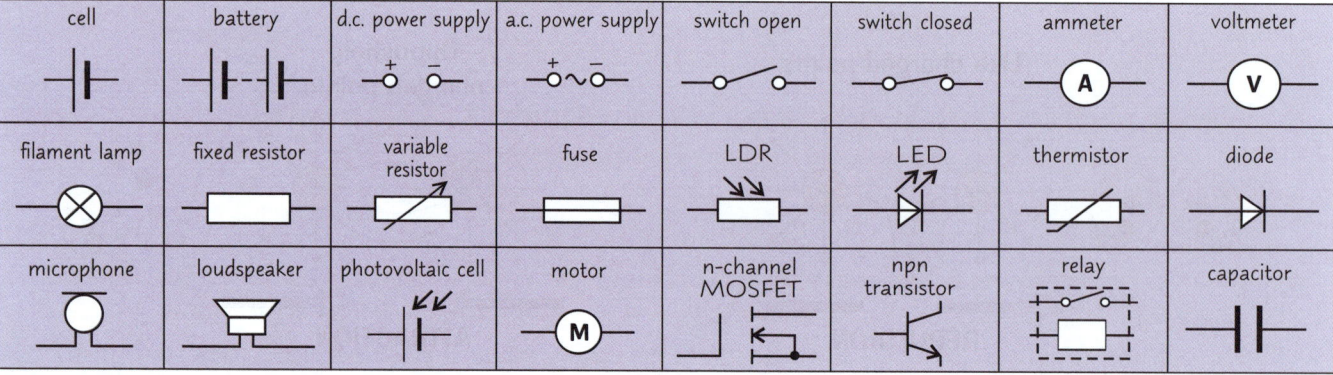

I think it's about time you took charge...

You've no doubt seen some of those circuit symbols before, but take a good look and practise drawing all of them.

Q1 A laptop charger passes a current of 8.0 A through a laptop battery. Calculate how long the charger needs to be connected to the battery for 28 800 C of charge to be transferred to the laptop. [3 marks]

Potential Difference and Resistance

Current is pushed around a circuit by a potential difference, and slowed down by resistance.

Energy is Transferred from Cells and Other Sources

1) Potential difference (or voltage) is the driving force that pushes the charge round. Its unit is the volt, V. One volt is one joule per coulomb (a coulomb is a measure of charge — p.38).
2) The potential difference (p.d.) of an electrical supply is defined as the amount of energy given to the charge carriers (electrons) per unit charge in a circuit.
3) The p.d. across a component is the energy transferred by each unit of charge.

Potential difference and voltage are the same thing.

Resistance Opposes the Flow of Current

1) The resistance of a component is a measure of how much it slows down the charge carriers in a circuit.
2) The greater the resistance across a component, the smaller the current that flows (for a given potential difference across the component).
3) Resistance is measured in ohms, Ω.

Resistance, Potential Difference and Current: $V = I \times R$

For potential difference (V) in volts, V, current (I) in amps, A, and resistance (R) in ohms, Ω:

| potential difference = current × resistance |

As a formula triangle: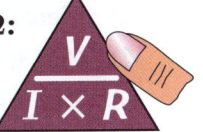

If you rearrange this equation, you can use it to calculate the resistance of a component from measurements of potential difference and current (e.g. from the experiment on the next page).

You can also measure resistance using an ohmmeter or a multimeter, by removing the component from the circuit and connecting it to the ohmmeter or multimeter.

EXAMPLE: A 4.0 Ω resistor in a circuit has a potential difference of 6.0 V across it. What is the current through the resistor?

1) State $V = IR$ and substitute in the values. $V = IR$ so $6.0 = I \times 4.0$
2) Rearrange to find the current. $I = 6.0 \div 4.0 = 1.5$ A

1) Since the current of a circuit is affected by its resistance, you can use a variable resistor to change the current of a supply instead of using a variable supply like the one on the next page.
2) If the resistance of a component is constant, then the potential difference across it is directly proportional to the current though it. The component is known as ohmic — it obeys Ohm's Law.
3) A resistor at a constant temperature is ohmic.

Resistance Increases with Temperature (Usually)

1) When an electrical charge flows through a component, it has to do work against resistance.
2) This causes an electrical transfer of energy (work done = energy transferred, p.24).
3) Some of this energy is converted to heat energy of the component and the surroundings. This causes the component to heat up.
4) The increase in temperature causes resistance to increase and so reduces the current that flows through the component. If the component gets too hot, no current will be able to flow.
5) A thermistor is an exception — the resistance decreases when the temperature increases (p.41).

In the end you'll have to learn this — resistance is futile...

$V = IR$ is one of the most useful equations in electricity — so have a quick practise before moving on.

Q1 A current of 4.0 A flows through a resistor which has a potential difference of 8.0 V across it. Calculate the resistance of the resistor. [3 marks]

PRACTICAL: Investigating Components

Ooh experiments, you've gotta love 'em. Here's a simple experiment for investigating different components.

The Standard Test Circuit

You can use this circuit to investigate the relationship between current (*I*), p.d. (*V*) and resistance (*R*) for a range of components. It contains:

- **Ammeter** — this measures the current (in amps) flowing through the component. It can be put anywhere in the main circuit but it must be placed in series (p.43) with the component, never in parallel.
- **Voltmeter** — this measures the potential difference across the component. It must be placed in parallel (p.44) with the component under test.

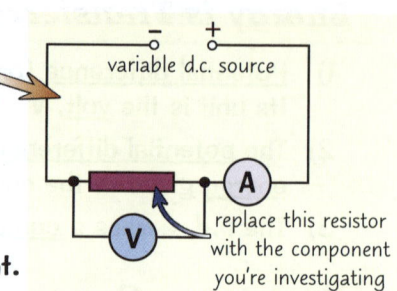

replace this resistor with the component you're investigating

You can Verify That a Resistor Obeys Ohm's Law

1) Connect the resistor in the circuit as shown above.
2) Change the output potential difference of the power supply. This alters the current flowing through the circuit and the potential difference across the component.
3) Measure several pairs of values for *I* and *V*.
4) Plot the current against the potential difference to get an *I-V* graph.
5) The graph will be a straight line graph through the origin — this verifies that the resistor obeys Ohm's Law, as the voltage is directly proportional to the current.
6) You can work out the resistance from the gradient — for an ohmic conductor the gradient is equal to $1 \div R$. *R* should stay the same because the resistor is ohmic.
7) Like with any experiment, you should take repeats and calculate a mean for each reading.
8) A resistor is only ohmic at a fixed temperature (p.39) so try to keep the temperature constant by using low currents and allowing the circuit to cool down between repeats.

You could also plot a V-I graph and the gradient would be equal to R.

Non-Ohmic Components give Curved I-V Graphs

1) You can use the circuit above to test whether any component is ohmic.
2) Ohmic components (like a resistor at a fixed temperature) have straight *I-V* graphs — resistance is fixed.
3) Non-ohmic components have a curved *I-V* graph — the resistance is not fixed.

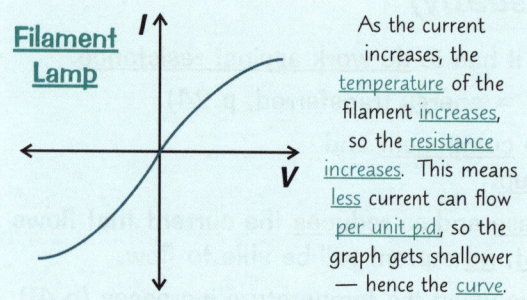

Filament Lamp

As the current increases, the temperature of the filament increases, so the resistance increases. This means less current can flow per unit p.d., so the graph gets shallower — hence the curve.

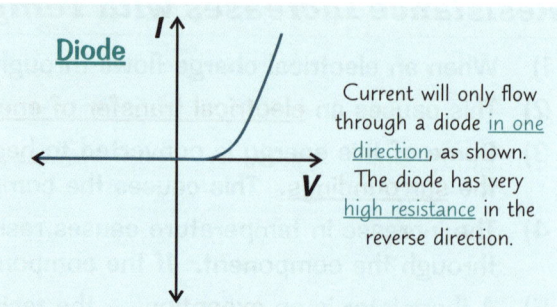

Diode

Current will only flow through a diode in one direction, as shown. The diode has very high resistance in the reverse direction.

Measure gymnastics — use a vaultmeter...

Make sure you can describe the experiment above — remember, ammeters in series, voltmeters in parallel.

Q1 Draw a circuit you could use to investigate whether a resistor is ohmic. [2 marks]

Circuit Devices

You've learnt all of the circuit symbols for circuit devices, now it's time to see how they all work...

LDR is Short for Light Dependent Resistor

1) An LDR is a resistor that is dependent on the intensity of light. Simple really.
2) In bright light, the resistance falls.
3) In darkness, the resistance is highest.
4) They have lots of applications including automatic night lights, outdoor lighting and burglar detectors.

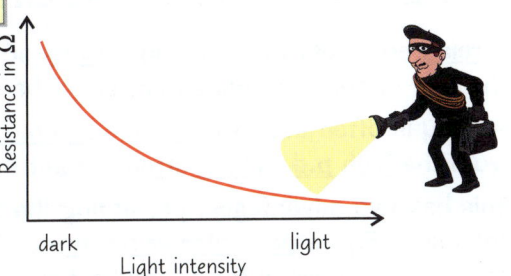

The Resistance of a Thermistor Depends on Temperature

1) A thermistor is a temperature dependent resistor.
2) In hot conditions, the resistance drops.
3) In cool conditions, the resistance goes up.
4) Thermistors make useful temperature detectors, e.g. car engine temperature sensors and electronic thermostats.

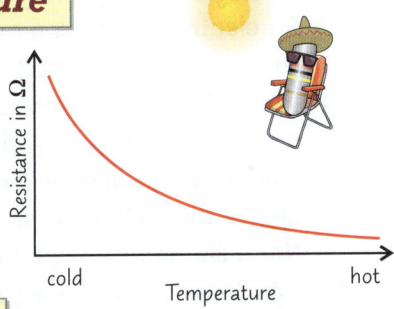

Current Only Flows in One Direction through a Diode

1) A diode is a special device made from a semiconductor material such as silicon.
2) It lets current flow freely through it in one direction, but not in the other (i.e. there's a very high resistance in the reverse direction).
3) This turns out to be really useful in various electronic circuits.

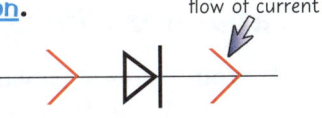

Light-Emitting Diodes are Very Useful

1) A light-emitting diode (LED) only emits light when a current flows through it in one direction.
2) LEDs are being used more and more as lighting, as they use a much smaller current than other forms of lighting.
3) LEDs indicate the presence of current in a circuit. They're often used in appliances (e.g. TVs) to show that they are switched on.
4) They're also used for the numbers on digital clocks, in traffic lights and in remote controls.

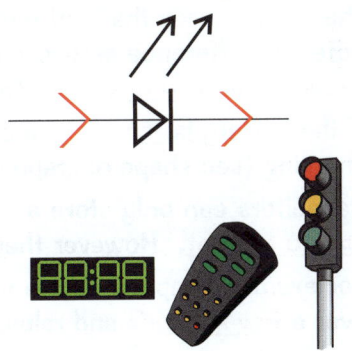

Photovoltaic Cells Convert Light Energy into Electrical Energy

1) Photovoltaic cells (solar cells) directly convert light energy from the Sun into electrical energy.
2) Small solar cells are sometimes used to power calculators. Larger arrays of solar cells are used to power some road signs, and even larger arrays can be used power satellites in orbit around Earth.

Permistors — resistance decreases with curliness of hair...

It's nice to know how different components are used in daily life — the next time your heating or your outdoor lighting turns on automatically, you can be smug in your knowledge of thermistors and LDRs.

Q1 Describe one everyday use for the following components:
   a) LDR   b) thermistor   [2 marks]

More Circuit Devices

Here's where it gets even trickier, go slowly over this page because these devices are much more complicated.

A Relay is a Switch that Uses an Electromagnet

1) A relay connects two isolated circuits so that when the first circuit is switched on, so is the second.
2) A relay is often used to isolate a low p.d., low current switch circuit from the high p.d., high current circuit that needs switching on.
3) This has two advantages, protecting the switch circuit and protecting the user. E.g. a car's starter motor needs a very high current, but the part you control (when you're turning the key) is in the low-current circuit — safely isolated by the relay.
4) A relay works by using an electromagnet called a relay coil. An electromagnet is a magnet that is only magnetic when an electric current flows through it.
5) When the switch in the low current circuit is closed, it turns on the electromagnet which generates a magnetic field.
6) The magnetic field causes a force of attraction which closes the switch in the high current circuit. Normally an iron contact is used to make this happen.
7) When the low current switch is opened, the electromagnet turns off and stops pulling. The high current switch opens and the high current circuit is broken again.

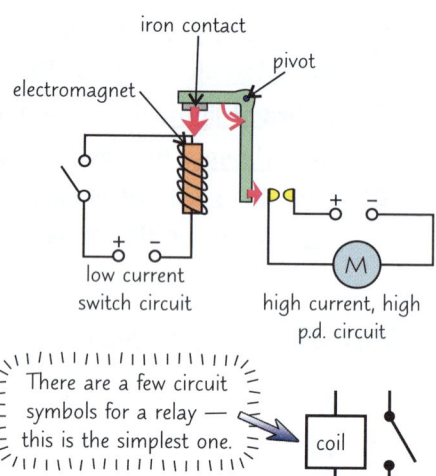

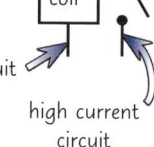

There are a few circuit symbols for a relay — this is the simplest one.

Capacitors Store Charge

1) You charge a capacitor by connecting it to a source of potential difference, e.g. a battery. As current flows around the circuit, charge gets stored on the capacitor.
2) The current decreases as you charge for longer periods of time.
3) The more charge that's stored on a capacitor, the larger the potential difference across it. When the potential difference across the capacitor is equal to that of the battery, the current stops and the capacitor is fully charged. The p.d. across the capacitor won't rise above the p.d. of the battery.
4) If the battery is removed, the capacitor discharges — the current is the same for discharging as for charging (see shape of graph above) but the current flows in the opposite direction round the circuit.
5) Capacitors can only store a small amount of charge, and they can't be used to provide a steady current. However they're very useful when you want to release a lot of charge very quickly.
6) For example, capacitors are used in camera flashes to store charge over a few seconds and release it almost instantly.

Loudspeakers, Microphones and Motors Convert Energy in Similar Ways

1) Loudspeakers turn electrical energy signals into the vibration of a cone in the speaker which produces sound waves. They convert electrical energy to sound energy.
2) Microphones are basically loudspeakers in reverse. Sound waves cause a diaphragm in the microphone to vibrate and the vibrations are converted to electrical signals. They convert sound energy to electrical energy.
3) A motor converts electrical energy to the kinetic energy of a rotating coil in the motor. Motors often waste energy as heat and sound energy.

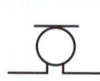
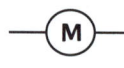

You should be relay proud of yourself...

You're nearly through all of the circuit devices. It'd be a good idea to go over each device again before moving on.

Q1 Name a circuit device that converts electrical energy into sound energy. [1 mark]

Section 3 — Electricity

Series Circuits

There's a difference between connecting components in series and parallel. Make sure you learn it, and know the rules about what happens to current, p.d. and resistance in each case — read on for more series fun.

Series Circuits — All or Nothing

1) In series circuits, the different components are connected in a line, end to end, between the +ve and –ve of the power supply (except for voltmeters, which are always connected in parallel, p.40, but they don't count as part of the circuit).

2) If you remove or disconnect one component, the circuit is broken and the components all stop working. This is generally not very handy, and in practice very few things are connected in series.

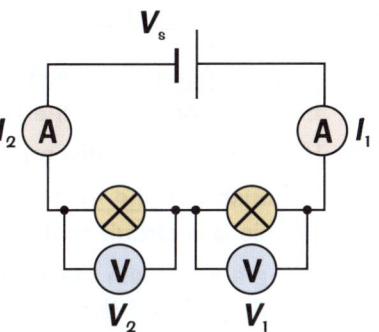

Potential Difference is Shared

In series circuits the total p.d. (V_s where s stands for series) of the supply is shared between the various components. So the potential differences round a series circuit always add up to equal the source p.d.:

Total p.d. in a series circuit
$$V_s = V_1 + V_2 + ...$$

Current is the Same Everywhere

1) In series circuits the same current (I_s) flows through all components:

2) The size of the current is determined by the total p.d. and the total resistance of the circuit: i.e. $I = V \div R$.

Total current in a series circuit
$$I_s = I_1 = I_2 = ...$$

Resistance Adds Up

1) In series circuits the total resistance, R_T, of two components is just the sum of their resistances:

$$R_T = R_1 + R_2 + ...$$

2) This is because by adding a resistor in series, the two resistors have to share the total p.d.

3) The potential difference across each resistor is lower, so the current through each resistor is also lower. In a series circuit, the current is the same everywhere so the current in the circuit is reduced when a resistor is added. This means the total resistance of the circuit increases.

4) The bigger a component's resistance, the bigger its share of the total potential difference.

EXAMPLE: For the circuit diagram below, calculate the current passing through the circuit.

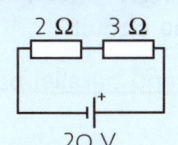

1) First find the total resistance by adding together the resistances of the two resistors.

$R_T = R_1 + R_2 = 2 + 3 = 5\ \Omega$

2) Then state $V = IR$ and substitute in the values you have. Rearrange to find I.

$V = IR$ so $20 = I \times 5$
$I = 20 \div 5 = 4$ A

Cell Potential Differences Add Up

1) There is a bigger p.d. when more cells are in series, if they're all connected the same way.

2) For example when two cells with a potential difference of 1.5 V are connected in series they supply 3 V in total.

Series circuits — they're no laughing matter...

Get those rules straightened out in your head, then have a quick go at this question to test what you can remember.

Q1 Two 12 V cells are connected in series with a 2 Ω resistor, a 3 Ω resistor and a 7 Ω resistor. Calculate the current through the circuit. [5 marks]

Parallel Circuits

Parallel circuits are more common in real life. All the electrics in your house will be wired in parallel circuits.

Parallel Circuits — Independence and Isolation

1) In parallel circuits, each component is separately connected to the +ve and −ve of the supply (except ammeters, p.40).
2) If you remove or disconnect one of them, it will hardly affect the others at all.
3) In houses, a ring main is used to connect all of the sockets together — this is a circuit that connects all sockets in parallel.
4) Using a ring main means that sockets can be switched on and off separately, and they all get the full 230 V of the electricity supply (see below).

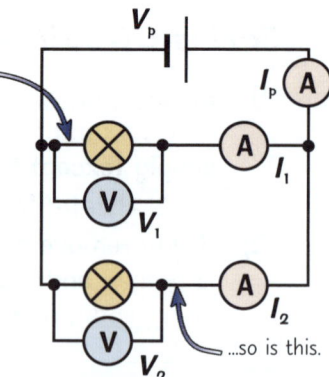

Potential Difference is the Same Across All Components

1) In parallel circuits all components get the full source p.d., so the potential difference is the same across all components.
2) This means that identical bulbs connected in parallel will all be at the same brightness.

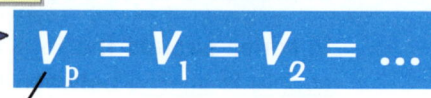

$$V_P = V_1 = V_2 = \ldots$$

Total p.d. in a parallel circuit

Current is Shared Between Branches

1) In parallel circuits the total current flowing around the circuit is equal to the total of all the currents through the separate components:
2) At the junctions where the current either splits or rejoins, the total current going in has to equal the total current leaving.
3) If two identical components are connected in parallel then the same current will flow through each component.

Total current in a parallel circuit

$$I_P = I_1 + I_2 + \ldots$$

The currant is shared between branches

Adding a Resistor in Parallel Reduces the Total Resistance

1) If you have two resistors in parallel, their total resistance, R_T, is less than the resistance of the smallest of the two resistors.

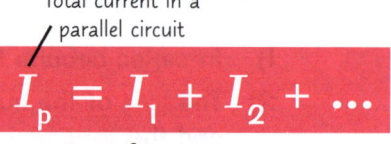

$$\frac{1}{R_T} = \frac{1}{R_1} + \frac{1}{R_2} + \ldots$$

- In parallel, both resistors have the same potential difference across them as the source.
- This means the 'pushing force' making the current flow is the same for each resistor added.
- But by adding another loop, the current has more than one direction to go in.
- This increases the total current that can flow around the circuit. Using $V = IR$, an increase in current means a decrease in the total resistance of the circuit.

2) You can combine the rules of the last two pages for circuits with series and parallel parts.

EXAMPLE: Calculate the total resistance of the circuit shown.

1) Calculate the total resistance of the two parallel resistors.
2) The two parallel resistors can now be treated as a single resistor of resistance 1.33... Ω.
3) Now add the two series resistances.

$$\frac{1}{R_T} = \frac{1}{R_1} + \frac{1}{R_2} = \frac{1}{2} + \frac{1}{4} = \frac{3}{4}$$
$$R_T = 4 \div 3 = 1.33\ldots$$

$$R_T = R_1 + R_2 = 3 + 1.33\ldots = 4 \text{ Ω (to 1 s.f.)}$$

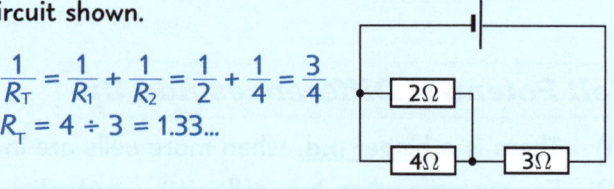

A current shared (between identical components) — is a current halved...

Parallel circuits are a bit more complicated but much more useful than series circuits, so get learning them.

Q1 Describe what happens to the current and resistance in a circuit containing a cell and a resistor when a second resistor is added in parallel. [2 marks]

Section 3 — Electricity

Potential Dividers

Potential dividers are pairs of resistors. They divide the p.d. in a circuit so you can get outputs of different p.d.

The Higher the Resistance, the Greater the P.d. Share

1) A p.d. across a pair of resistors is 'shared out' according to their relative resistances.
2) The larger the share of the total resistance, the larger the share of the total p.d.

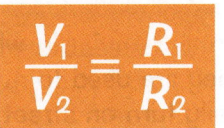

$$\frac{V_1}{V_2} = \frac{R_1}{R_2}$$

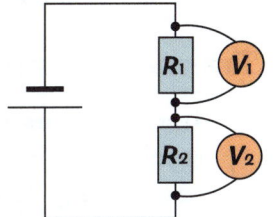

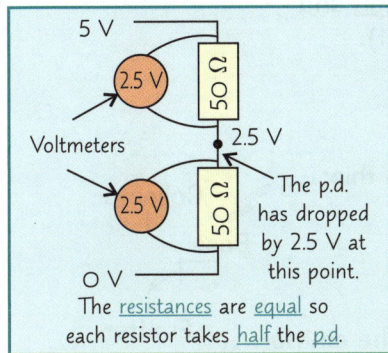

The resistances are equal so each resistor takes half the p.d.

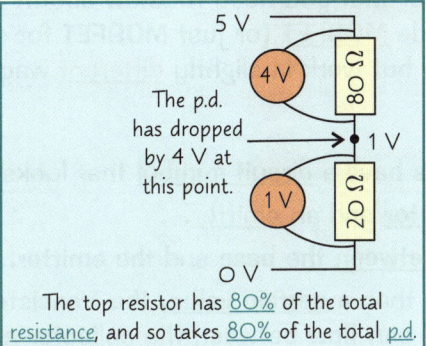

The top resistor has 80% of the total resistance, and so takes 80% of the total p.d.

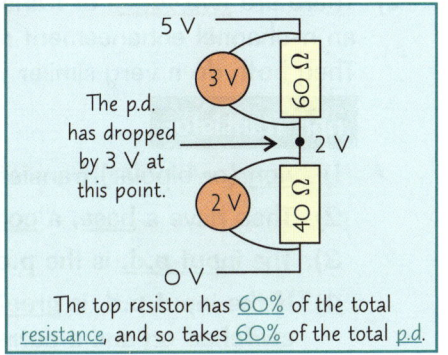

The top resistor has 60% of the total resistance, and so takes 60% of the total p.d.

Potential Dividers are Quite Useful

1) Potential dividers allow you to run a device that requires a certain p.d. from a battery of a different potential difference.
2) Putting the device across the resistor R_2 allows it to run off a p.d. of V_2 when the source has a p.d. of V_s. This is the formula you need:

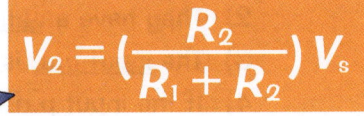

$$V_2 = \left(\frac{R_2}{R_1 + R_2}\right) V_s$$

EXAMPLE: In the diagram, the source p.d. for the potential divider is 9 V. R_1 is 20 Ω and R_2 is 40 Ω. What is the output p.d. across R_2?

$V_2 = \left(\frac{R_2}{R_1 + R_2}\right) V_s = \left(\frac{40}{20 + 40}\right) \times 9 = 6$ V

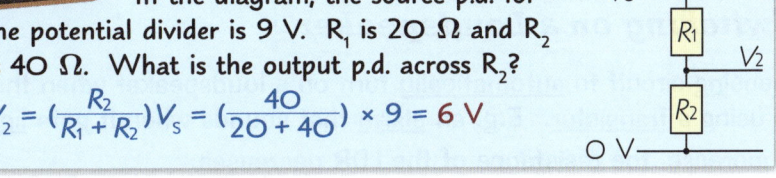

3) The output p.d. (V_2) depends on the relative values of R_1 and R_2.
4) From the formula, you should see that if R_2 is very big compared to R_1, the bit in the brackets cancels down to about 1, so V_2 is approximately V_s. But if R_2 is a lot smaller than R_1, the bit in brackets becomes so small that V_2 is approximately 0.
5) If R_1 is a variable resistor, you can change V_2 to any value between 0 and V_s.

Potential Dividers with LDRs or Thermistors Make Sensing Circuits

1) Potential dividers can be turned into sensing circuits. These can be used to increase the power to components (or even turn them on if a transistor is used, see next page) depending on the conditions that they are in.
2) The circuit on the right is a sensing circuit in a room.
3) As the room gets hotter, the resistance of the thermistor decreases and it takes a smaller share of the p.d. from the power supply. So the p.d. across the fixed resistor and the fan rises, making the fan go faster.
4) You can use a similar setup for a sensing circuit containing an LDR.

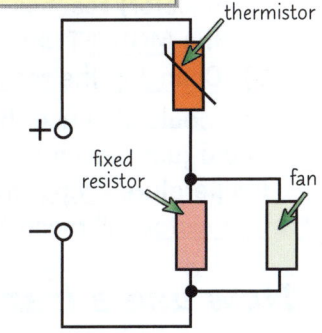

My boyfriend's mother is a potential divider...

You'll be given these equations in the exam, but you still need to know how to use them.

Q1 Calculate the potential difference across the 6 Ω resistor in the diagram. [3 marks]

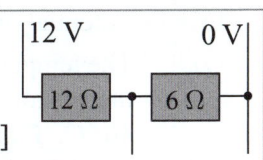

Section 3 — Electricity

Transistors

Transistors are the basic building blocks of electronic components.
They can be made so small that the circuits of a modern computer may contain billions of them.

Transistors are Electronic Switches

1) Transistors are switched on automatically when their input potential difference reaches a certain level. They are used to automatically control electronic circuits, e.g. to automatically turn on street lights when it gets dark.

2) There are two types of transistor that you need to know about: an npn and an n-channel enhancement mode MOSFET (or just MOSFET for short). They both do a very similar job but work in slightly different ways.

npn Transistor

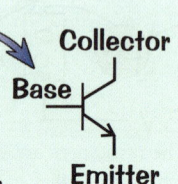

1) npn (or bipolar) transistors have a circuit symbol that looks like this:
2) They have a base, a collector and an emitter.
3) The input p.d. is the p.d between the base and the emitter.
4) If the input p.d. is greater than a certain value, the transistor is switched on and a current can flow between the collector and the emitter.

MOSFET Transistor

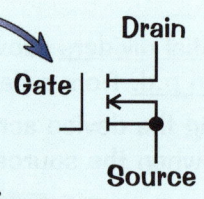

1) MOSFET transistors have a circuit symbol that looks like this:
2) They have a gate, a drain and a source.
3) The input p.d. is the p.d between gate and the source.
4) If the input p.d. is greater than a certain value, the transistor is switched on and a current can flow between the source and the drain.

Example — Switching on a Loudspeaker

You can make a sensing circuit to automatically turn on a loudspeaker when the light level reaches a certain brightness using a transistor. E.g. an alarm that sounds when it gets light in the morning.

1) As light levels increase, the resistance of the LDR decreases.
2) This means that the potential difference across the variable resistor increases.
3) This happens because the LDR and variable resistor together act like a potential divider — if the variable resistor has a larger share of the resistance, it also has a larger share of the potential difference.
4) When the input p.d. (the p.d. across the variable resistor) reaches a certain value, it switches on the MOSFET and turns on the loudspeaker.
5) Changing the resistance of the variable resistor determines the light level at which the speaker turns on.

You could also use this system to turn on a heater when the temperature in a room drops too low. You'd just have a potential divider system with a thermistor and a variable resistor. When the temperature drops, the resistance of the thermistor increases. Putting the transistor across the thermistor will mean the transistor turns on as the temperature drops, turning on the heater.

Now use a transistor to automatically start revising...

It's really important that you totally get how transistors play a part in automatic circuits that include potential dividers with thermistors or LDRs. Examiners love these circuits.

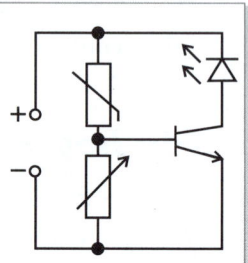

Q1   The temperature of an oven hob is monitored for safety by a circuit containing a thermistor. An LED is automatically switched on when the temperature is above 40 °C. Explain how the circuit operates to switch on the LED.   [3 marks]

Section 3 — Electricity

Mains Electricity

Electric current is the <u>electrical charge transferred</u>. To transfer energy, it <u>doesn't matter which way</u> the charge electrons are going. That's why an <u>alternating current</u> works. Read on to find out more...

a.c. is Alternating, d.c. is Direct

1) There are two types of <u>electric current</u> — <u>alternating</u> current (a.c.) and <u>direct</u> current (d.c.).
2) In <u>a.c. supplies</u> the current is <u>constantly</u> changing direction. <u>Alternating currents</u> are produced by <u>alternating potential differences</u> in which the <u>positive</u> and <u>negative</u> ends of the p.d. keep <u>alternating</u>.
3) Alternating currents have a <u>frequency</u>. Frequency is the number of times the current <u>changes direction and back</u> per second, measured in hertz, Hz.
4) <u>Direct current</u> is a current that is always flowing in the <u>same direction</u>.
5) The frequency of d.c. current is <u>zero</u> — it <u>never</u> changes direction.

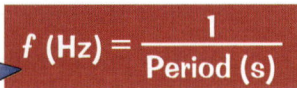

$$f\,(\text{Hz}) = \frac{1}{\text{Period (s)}}$$

Mains Supply is a.c., Battery Supply is d.c.

1) The UK mains supply is an <u>a.c.</u> supply at approximately <u>230 volts</u>.
2) The frequency of the a.c. mains supply is <u>50 cycles per second</u> or <u>50 Hz</u> (hertz).
3) By contrast, cells and batteries supply <u>direct current</u> (d.c.)

Electricity Supplies Can Be Shown on an Oscilloscope Screen

1) A <u>cathode ray oscilloscope</u> (CRO) is basically a snazzy <u>voltmeter</u>.
2) If you plug an <u>a.c. supply</u> into an oscilloscope, you get a '<u>trace</u>' on the screen that shows how the potential difference of the supply changes with <u>time</u>. The trace goes up and down in a <u>regular pattern</u> — some of the time it's positive and some of the time it's negative.
3) If you plug in a <u>d.c. supply</u>, the trace you get is just a <u>straight line</u>.
4) The <u>vertical height</u> of the a.c. trace at any point shows the <u>input p.d.</u> at that point.
5) For d.c. it's a <u>lot simpler</u> — the p.d. is just the distance from the <u>straight line trace</u> to the centre line.

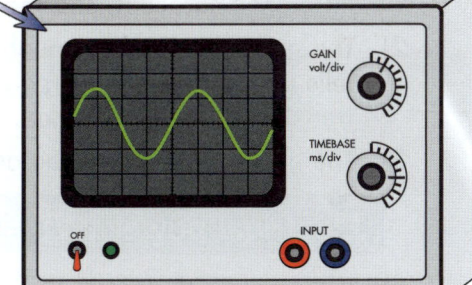

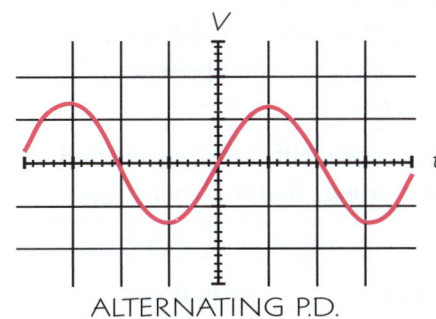
ALTERNATING P.D.

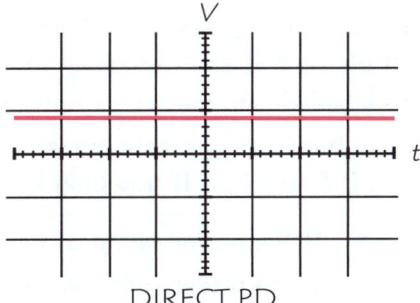
DIRECT P.D.

6) You can connect an oscilloscope to a <u>data logging system</u> to record the a.c. and d.c. traces — the trace on a data logger looks <u>exactly the same</u> as an oscilloscope trace.

I wish my bank account had a gain dial...

Make sure you can do a sketch to show how the potential difference changes with time for a.c. and d.c. supplies.

Q1   Explain the difference between alternating current and direct current.   [2 marks]

Power

Electrical devices transfer energy and their power determines how quickly this happens.

Energy Transferred Depends on Power

1) The power of an appliance is the electrical energy that it transfers per second:

   Power (W) = Energy transferred (J) ÷ Time (s)

   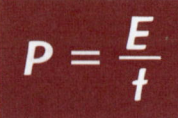
   $$P = \frac{E}{t}$$

2) Appliances are often given a power rating — they're labelled with the maximum safe power that they can operate at. You can usually take this to be their maximum operating power.

3) The power rating tells you the maximum amount of energy transferred per second when the appliance is in use.

EXAMPLE: A 600 W microwave is used for 5 minutes. How long (in minutes) would a 750 W microwave take to transfer the same amount of energy?

1) State the equation for power, energy and time. $P = E \div t$
2) Substitute in and rearrange to calculate the energy transferred by the 600 W microwave in five minutes. $600 = E \div (5 \times 60)$ so $E = 600 \times (5 \times 60)$ = 180 000 J
3) Sub in the energy you calculated and the power of the 750 W microwave and rearrange again to find t. $750 = 180\,000 \div t$ so $t = 180\,000 \div 750$ = 240 s
4) Convert the time back to minutes. $240 \div 60 = 4$ minutes

Remember that the time must be in seconds when you use the equation.

Power Also Depends on Current and Potential Difference

1) The power transferred by an appliance depends on the potential difference across it, and the current flowing through it.

2) The p.d. tells you how much energy each unit of charge transfers (p.39), and the current tells you how much charge passes per unit time. So both will affect the rate that energy is transferred to an appliance, and the rate at which it transfers energy to other types.

3) The power of an appliance can be found with:

   Electrical power (W) = Current (A) × Potential difference (V) $P = IV$

4) If the power that an appliance is operating at goes above its power rating, the appliance could be dangerous (e.g. it could cause a fire). Fuses are used to make sure this doesn't happen.

5) Power depends on current and potential difference. Mains electricity is fixed at 230 V, so if the power gets higher the current will too.

6) A fuse is a component which contains a strip of metal that will melt if the current through it gets too high — breaking the circuit and turning off the appliance.

7) Fuses are labelled with the current at which they'll melt.

8) If you know the maximum safe current, just choose a fuse with a higher current value. Fuses are usually 3 A or 13 A. If you only know the power rating, follow these rules:

   - If the power rating of the appliance is below 720 W, a 3 A fuse is used.
   - If the power rating is above 720 W then a 13 A fuse is used.

9) You can also find the power if you know the resistance and either the potential difference or the current. To do this, stick $V = IR$ and $I = V \div R$ from page 39 into $P = IV$. This gives you two equations:

   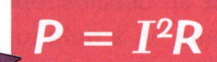
   $P = I^2R$ $P = \dfrac{V^2}{R}$

You have the power — now use your potential...

I'm afraid the best way to learn all of this is to just practise using those equations again and again. Sorry.

Q1 Calculate the resistance of a 55 W light bulb connected to a 230 V mains supply. [3 marks]

Section 3 — Electricity

Revision Questions for Section 3

Well, that wraps up Section 3 — electricity is my least favourite part of physics, but sadly it's on the exam.
- Try these questions and tick off each one when you get it right.
- When you've done all the questions for a topic and are completely happy with it, tick off the topic.

Charge, Current, Potential Difference and Resistance (p.37-40) ☑

1) True or false? A positively charged particle between two oppositely charged parallel plates travels from negative to positive.
2) Draw the path that a positively charged particle takes near a single negative point charge.
3) Define electrical current and state an equation that links current, charge and time.
4) Draw the circuit symbols for: a cell, a filament lamp, a diode, a fuse and an LDR.
5) What is meant by potential difference and resistance of a component?
6) What is the equation that links potential difference, current and resistance?
7) What is an ohmic conductor?
8) Describe an experiment that could be used to verify that a resistor obeys Ohm's Law.
9) Sketch an I-V graph for an ohmic resistor.

Circuit Devices (p.41-42) ☑

10) Describe how the resistance of an LDR varies with light intensity.
11) What happens to the resistance of a thermistor as it gets hotter?
12) What is a diode?
13) Explain how a relay coil in a circuit causes a switch in another circuit to close.
14) Describe the function of a capacitor.
15) What is the overall energy change that occurs in a microphone?

Series and Parallel Circuits (p.43-44) ☑

16) True or false? Potential difference is shared between components in a series circuit.
17) How does the current through each component vary in a series circuit?
18) How does potential difference vary between components connected in parallel?
19) Explain why adding resistors in parallel decreases the total resistance of a circuit.

More Circuit Devices (p.45-46) ☑

20) Explain how potential dividers can be used to run a component that requires a low p.d. from a high p.d. source.
21) Explain what each term represents in the equation for the output p.d. of a potential divider.
22) Draw the circuit symbol for a MOSFET transistor.
23) Describe how a circuit containing a transistor be used as a switch.
24) Explain how you would use a thermistor, a variable resistor and a transistor to make a light switch on when the light level in a room drops.

Electricity and Power (p.47-48) ☑

25) Sketch the potential difference-time trace you would see on a CRO screen for an a.c. supply.
26) Define power in terms of energy transferred.
27) What is the power rating of an appliance?
28) State three equations for electrical power involving current, resistance or potential difference.

Section 4 — Properties of Matter

The Kinetic Model and Temperature

According to the kinetic model, everything's made of tiny particles. The table, this book, your Gran...

The Kinetic Model is a Way of Explaining Matter Involving Particles

1) In the kinetic model, you can think of the particles that make up matter as tiny balls. You can explain the ways that matter behaves in terms of how these particles move, and the forces between them.

2) Three states of matter are solid (e.g. ice), liquid (e.g. water) and gas (e.g. water vapour). The particles of a substance in each state are the same — only the arrangement and energy of the particles are different. If you reverse a change of state, the particles go back to how they were before.

3) So changes of state are physical changes (only the form of a substance changes).

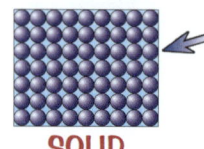
SOLID

Strong forces of attraction hold the particles in a solid close together in a fixed, regular arrangement. The particles don't have much kinetic energy so they can only vibrate about their fixed positions.

The forces of attraction between the particles in a liquid are weaker than in a solid. The particles are close together, but can move past each other and form irregular arrangements. They have more kinetic energy than the particles in a solid — they move in random directions at low speeds.

LIQUID

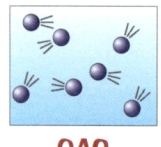
GAS

There are almost no forces of attraction between the particles in a gas. Particles have more kinetic energy than those in liquids and are free to move — they travel in random directions at high speeds.

4) When you heat a substance, the heat energy (or thermal energy) is absorbed by the particles, making them move or vibrate faster. This causes either a rise in temperature, or, if the particles have enough energy to overcome the forces of attraction between them, a change in state like melting or boiling.

5) If you decrease the temperature of something, you're reducing the kinetic energy of the particles — they move about more slowly or vibrate less. This can cause condensing or freezing if the particles no longer have enough energy to overcome the forces of attraction between them.

6) So... **Temperature is a measure of the mean kinetic energy of the particles of a substance.**

Absolute Zero is as Cold as Stuff Can Get — 0 Kelvin

1) In theory, the coldest that anything can ever get is −273 °C — this temperature is known as absolute zero. At absolute zero, the particles have as little kinetic energy as it's possible to have — they're pretty much still.

2) Absolute zero is the start of the Kelvin scale of temperature — 0 K.

3) 0 K = −273 °C and a temperature change of 1 °C is also a change of 1 kelvin. The two scales are pretty similar — the only difference is where the zero occurs.

4) To convert from degrees Celsius to kelvins, just add 273.
And to convert from kelvins to degrees Celsius, just subtract 273.

Brownian Motion Supports the Kinetic Model

1) Large particles suspended in a liquid or gas, such as smoke particles in air, move with Brownian motion.

2) This is a random, jerky motion. The suspended particles move in this way because they are being bombarded by smaller, lighter particles (e.g. air molecules) which are travelling at high speeds.

Absolute zero — the coolest part of physics...

Remember, the greater the temperature of a substance, the more kinetic energy the particles have on average.

Q1   Ethanol boils at 78 °C. Calculate this value in kelvin.   [1 mark]

Specific Heat Capacity

The temperature of something isn't the same as its heat energy. That's where specific heat capacity comes in.

Specific Heat Capacity Relates Temperature and Energy

1) It takes more energy to increase the temperature of some materials than others. E.g. you need 4180 J to warm 1 kg of water by 1 °C, but only 128 J to warm 1 kg of lead by 1 °C.

2) Materials that need to gain lots of energy to warm up also release loads of energy when they cool down again. They store a lot of energy for a given change in temperature.

3) The change in the heat energy of a substance when you heat it is related to the change in its temperature by its specific heat capacity. The specific heat capacity of a substance is the amount of heat energy needed to raise the temperature of 1 kg of a substance by 1 °C:

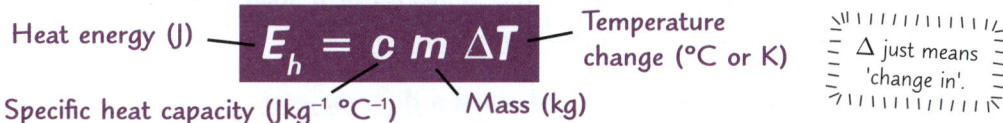

$$E_h = c \, m \, \Delta T$$

Heat energy (J) — E_h
Specific heat capacity (Jkg^{-1} °C^{-1}) — c
Mass (kg) — m
Temperature change (°C or K) — ΔT

Δ just means 'change in'.

4) In the exam, the question or the data sheet will list any specific heat capacities you need.

You can Find the Specific Heat Capacity of a Substance

You can use this experiment to find the specific heat capacity of a substance (solid or liquid). You should use thermal insulation to reduce the energy wasted to the surroundings.
This is how you can find the specific heat capacity of water, or any liquid:

1) Use a mass balance to measure the mass of the insulating container.
2) Fill the container with water and measure the mass again. The difference in mass is the mass of the water in the container.
3) Set up the experiment as shown — make sure the joulemeter reads zero and place a lid on the container if you have one.
4) Measure the temperature of the water, then turn on the power supply.
5) Keep an eye on the thermometer. When the temperature has increased by e.g. 10 degrees, stop the experiment and record the energy on the joulemeter, and the increase in temperature.
6) You can then calculate the specific heat capacity by rearranging the equation above.

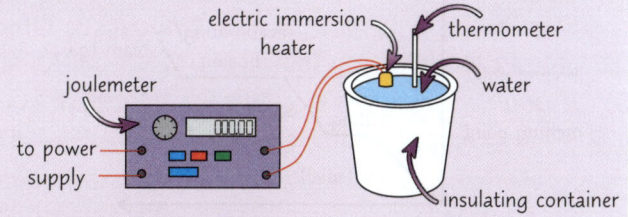

PRACTICAL

For a solid, you would replace the insulating container of water with a block of the solid with two holes in it for the heater and thermometer.

Conservation of Energy Applies to Heating

1) Conservation of energy says that energy can never be created or destroyed (p.24).
2) So when a substance is heated, all of the energy supplied increases the heat energy of either the substance or the surroundings — the energy transferred to the surroundings is 'wasted'.

Energy supplied = heat energy increase of substance + heat energy increase of surroundings

3) You might be expected to use the equation for power (the rate of energy transfer) in situations where a substance is heated or cooled. It is $P = E_h \div t$, p.48.

My specific eat capacity — 24 pies...

Make sure you practise using that specific heat capacity equation — it's a bit of a tricky one.

Q1 A metal has a specific heat capacity of 420 Jkg^{-1} °C^{-1}. Calculate how much the temperature of a 0.20 kg block of the metal will increase by if 1680 J of energy is supplied to it. [3 marks]

Specific Latent Heat

If you heat up a pan of water on the stove, the water never gets any hotter than 100 °C. You can carry on heating it, but the temperature won't rise. How come, you say? It's all to do with latent heat...

You Need to Put In Energy to Break Intermolecular Bonds

1) Remember, when you heat a solid or liquid, you're transferring energy to the particles in the substance. Most of the time this makes them vibrate or move faster (p.50). This is an increase in the mean kinetic energy of the particles, so the temperature increases.

2) However, when a substance is melting or boiling, you're still putting in energy, but it's used for breaking intermolecular bonds rather than raising the temperature.

3) When a substance is condensing or freezing, bonds are forming between particles, which releases energy. This means the temperature doesn't go down until all the substance has turned into a liquid (condensing) or a solid (freezing).

4) You can see this by doing this simple demonstration:

   1) Fill a beaker with crushed ice and place a thermometer into the beaker to record the temperature of the ice.
   2) Using the Bunsen burner, gradually heat the beaker full of ice.
   3) Every twenty seconds, record the temperature.
   4) Continue this process until the water begins to boil.
   5) Plot a graph of temperature against time for your experiment.

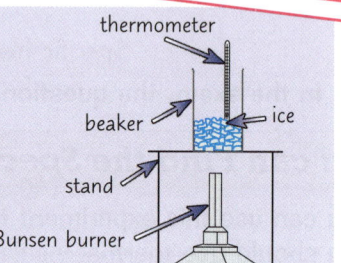

Your graph should look like this:

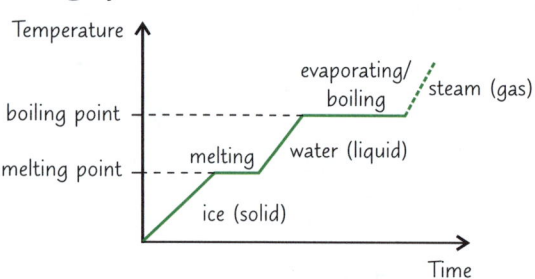

You get a similar one for condensing and freezing:

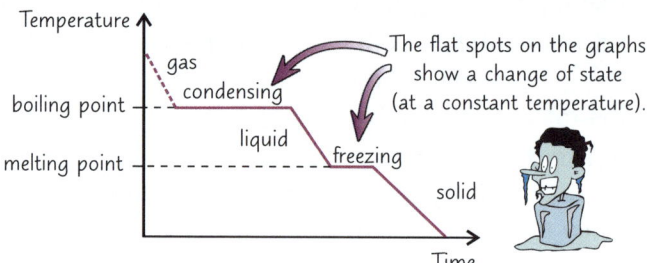

The flat spots on the graphs show a change of state (at a constant temperature).

5) The dotted lines show how the gas temperature would change if the gas was heated or cooled.

Specific Latent Heat is the Energy Needed to Change State

1) The specific latent heat of a substance is the amount of energy needed to change 1 kg of it from one state to another without changing its temperature.
2) For cooling, specific latent heat is the energy released by a change in state.
3) Specific latent heat is different for different materials, and for changing between different states.
4) The specific latent heat for changing between a solid and a liquid (melting or freezing) is called the specific latent heat of fusion. The specific latent heat for changing between a liquid and a gas (evaporating, boiling or condensing) is called the specific latent heat of vaporisation.
5) You can work out the energy needed (or released) when a substance of mass m changes state:

$$\text{Heat energy} = \text{Mass} \times \text{Specific latent heat} \qquad E_h = ml$$

You're given values for the specific latent heat on the data sheet in the exam. Be careful to pick correctly out of fusion and vaporisation.

Heat energy is given in joules (J), mass is in kg and specific latent heat is in Jkg^{-1}.

Breaking Bonds — Blofeld never quite manages it...

Remember, when there's a change of state, there's no change in temperature.

Q1 Sketch a graph showing how the temperature of a sample of water will change over time as it is heated from –5 °C to 105 °C.

[3 marks]

Pressure

Gas particles fly around, bump into things and exert forces on them. This is happening to you right now — the air around you is exerting pressure on you (unless you're somehow reading this in space).

Pressure is the Force per Unit Area

The following equation can be used to calculate the pressure of solids, liquids and gases:

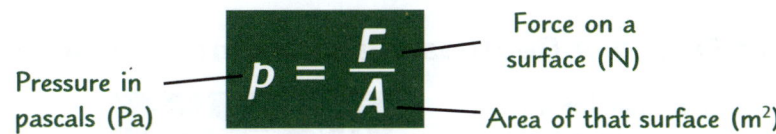

Pressure in pascals (Pa) — $p = \dfrac{F}{A}$ — Force on a surface (N), Area of that surface (m²)

EXAMPLE: Calculate the pressure exerted by a 20 N force over an area of 5 m². Substitute the values you're given into $p = F \div A$. $p = F \div A = 20 \div 5 = 4$ Pa

Colliding Gas Particles Create Pressure

1) According to the kinetic model (p.50), all matter is made up of very small, constantly moving particles.
2) Particles in a gas hardly take up any space. Most of the gas is empty space.
3) As the gas particles move about at high speeds, they bang into each other and whatever else happens to get in the way. When they collide with something, they exert a force (and so a pressure) on it.
4) In a sealed container, the outward gas pressure is the total force exerted by all of the particles in the gas on a unit area of the container walls.

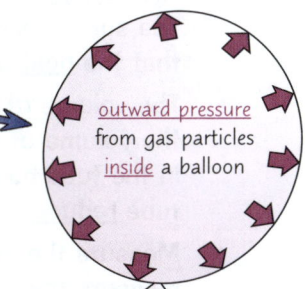

outward pressure from gas particles inside a balloon

Remember, temperature is a measure of the mean kinetic energy of the particles in a substance, see page 50.

Gas Pressure Varies with Volume and Temperature

1) The speed of gas particles depends on the temperature of the gas.
2) The higher the temperature, the more kinetic energy the particles have and the faster they move. This means they collide with the container more often and harder, so the force exerted on the container increases as the temperature increases.
3) So increasing the temperature of a fixed volume of gas increases its pressure.
4) Alternatively, if temperature is constant, increasing the volume of a gas means the particles get more spread out and hit the walls of the container less often. The gas pressure decreases.
5) The relationships between the temperature, volume and pressure of a gas are called the gas laws, and are covered in more detail on the next three pages.

Gas particles need to watch where they're going...

Remember, the more gas particles there are in a fixed volume, and the faster they travel, the higher the pressure...

Q1   A book has a length of 0.20 m and a width of 0.12 m. The weight of the book is 6.0 N. Calculate the pressure exerted by the book if it is placed onto a flat smooth surface.   [3 marks]

Q2   A syringe is sealed at one end and the plunger is pushed until the force exerted on it is 300 N. The area of the plunger is 20×10^{-4} m². Calculate the pressure of the trapped air on the plunger. [3 marks]

Section 4 — Properties of Matter

Gas Laws — Boyle's Law

Laws for gases? Whatever next?... I give it about 5 minutes before the no-win no-fee lawyers start calling you.

Gas Laws only work for a Fixed Mass of Gas

1) There are three gas laws coming up. They each apply only to closed systems.
2) A closed system means no particles can get in or out, so the mass of the gas is fixed.

Boyle's Law: Pressure Decreases as Volume Increases

1) Boyle's Law states that for a fixed mass of gas at a constant temperature: $p_1V_1 = p_2V_2$
2) Increasing the volume from V_1 to V_2 means the pressure decreases from p_1 to p_2. Pressure × volume remains constant.
3) Mathematically speaking, pressure and volume are inversely proportional — a graph of pressure against volume looks like this.
4) You can also show this relationship by plotting a graph of pressure against $1 \div V$ to get straight line through the origin.
5) You can investigate the effect of changing volume on pressure with this experiment:

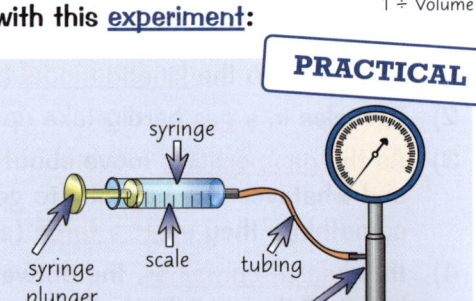

PRACTICAL

- The syringe is sealed so that it contains a fixed mass of air. The syringe should also be clamped (rather than held) so that the heat of your hand doesn't warm up the air.
- The volume of the tubing must be much smaller than the volume of the syringe because the volume of air in the tube hasn't been measured. Having a small tube reduces the uncertainty in the experiment.
- Measure the volume of air using the scale on the syringe and measure the pressure of the air using the pressure gauge.
- Slowly decrease the volume of air in the syringe by pushing in the plunger. Doing this slowly makes sure the temperature remains constant.
- Take measurements of both pressure and volume of air at sensible intervals.
- Plot a graph of p against $1 \div V$ to get a graph with a straight line through the origin. This shows that pressure is inversely proportional to volume and that Boyle's Law is correct.

If your graph doesn't go through the origin you may need to subtract atmospheric pressure from the pressure readings, see page 77.

6) These results can be explained using the kinetic model. Pushing the plunger in reduces the volume of gas inside the syringe. This means that the particles are closer together and collide with the inside of the syringe more often, exerting a larger total force. Because $p = F \div A$ (see previous page), a bigger force per unit area means the pressure measured by the gauge increases.

A weather balloon is filled with 8.0 m³ of helium gas at a pressure of 100 000 Pa. As the balloon rises, the pressure decreases to 50 000 Pa. Calculate the new volume of the balloon. Assume the temperature is constant.

1) State the equation for Boyle's Law and substitute in the values given.
2) Rearrange to find V_2.

$p_1V_1 = p_2V_2$ so 100 000 × 8.0 = 50 000 × V_2

V_2 = (100 000 × 8.0) ÷ 50 000 = 16 m³

Gas law number 301 — he who smelt it dealt it...

Make sure you understand how the kinetic theory of gases relates to this gas law before moving on to the next one.

Q1 Describe an experiment you could carry out to verify Boyle's Law. [3 marks]

Gas Laws — Gay-Lussac's Law

I wish these physicists would stop making so many laws... time for another one.

Gay-Lussac's Law: Pressure Increases as Temperature Increases

1) Gay-Lussac's Law states that for a fixed mass of gas at a constant volume:

   Temperature must be in kelvin for this equation to work — to convert from °C to K, just add 273 (see p.50).

   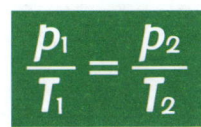
   $$\frac{p_1}{T_1} = \frac{p_2}{T_2}$$

2) Increasing the temperature from T_1 to T_2 means the pressure increases from p_1 to p_2. Pressure ÷ temperature remains constant.

3) Mathematically speaking, pressure and temperature in kelvin (p.50) are directly proportional — a graph of pressure against temperature looks like this.

4) You can investigate the effect of changing temperature on pressure by setting up this experiment:

PRACTICAL

- Immerse a flask of air sealed with a stopper in a beaker of water and heat gently until the water is near boiling. As much as possible of the flask should be submerged.
- Connect the stopper to a pressure gauge using a short length of tube.
- The volume of the tubing must be much smaller than the volume of the flask because the temperature of the air in the tubing is not being changed. Having a small tube reduces the uncertainty in the experiment.
- Record the temperature of the air and the pressure on the gauge.
- Allow the water to cool and, as it does so, regularly record the pressure on the gauge and the temperature of the air.
- Convert values of temperature in °C to in kelvin by adding 273.
- Plot your results on a graph of pressure against temperature in kelvin. If you draw a line of best fit, it should be a straight line through the origin. This shows that the pressure of the air is directly proportional to the temperature, which agrees with Gay-Lussac's Law.

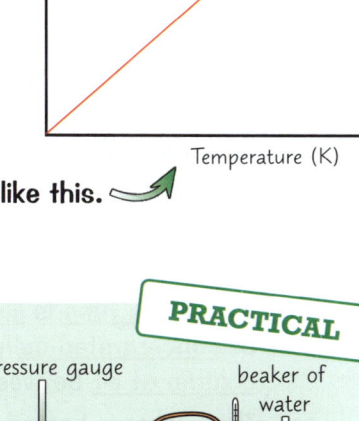

5) These results can be explained using the kinetic model. As the gas in the flask cools, the particles lose kinetic energy and move more slowly. Because the volume of the flask remains constant, the particles collide with the walls of the flask less often and so there is a smaller total force on the flask walls.

6) Also, because the particles are moving more slowly, they don't hit the flask walls as hard and exert a smaller force with each collision.

7) A smaller force on the walls of the flask per unit area decreases the pressure ($p = F ÷ A$, p.53).

EXAMPLE:  The gas in an aerosol can is at a pressure of 350 000 Pa at 293 K. Calculate the pressure of the gas in the can if it is heated to 323 K.

1) State the equation for Gay-Lussac's Law and substitute in the values.

   $p_1 ÷ T_1 = p_2 ÷ T_2$ so $350\,000 ÷ 293 = p_2 ÷ 323$

2) Rearrange to find p_2.

   $p_2 = (350\,000 ÷ 293) × 323$
   $= 385\,836.1... = 390\,000$ Pa (to 2 s.f.)

Don't feel under pressure — take some time to chill out...

Remember, each law involves two variables — the third must be kept constant. Gay-Lussac's Law is to do with pressure and temperature, so this means that the volume of the gas must be constant for the law to work.

Q1 A container contains gas at 350 K with a pressure of 25 000 Pa. Calculate by how much the temperature of the gas needs to increase for the pressure to reach 55 000 Pa. The mass and volume are fixed. [4 marks]

Gas Laws — Charles' Law and The Ideal Law

Just one more gas law to go and then you'll have learned all there is to ever know about gases... maybe.

Charles' Law: Volume Increases as Temperature Increases

1) Charles' Law states that for a fixed mass of gas at a constant pressure:

$$\frac{V_1}{T_1} = \frac{V_2}{T_2}$$

Temperature must be in kelvin (see p.50).

2) Increasing the temperature from T_1 to T_2 means the volume increases from V_1 to V_2. Volume ÷ temperature remains constant.
3) Mathematically speaking, temperature in kelvin and volume are directly proportional — a graph of volume against temperature in kelvin looks like this.
4) You can investigate the effect of changing temperature on volume with this experiment:

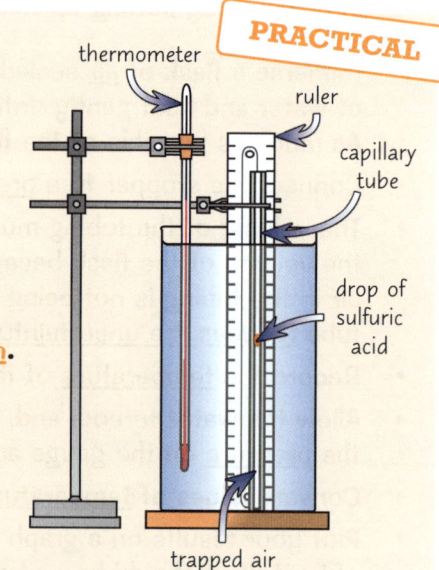

PRACTICAL

- A capillary tube is sealed at the bottom and contains a drop of concentrated sulfuric acid halfway up it — this traps a column of air between the bottom of the tube and the acid drop.
- The beaker is heated until the water is near-boiling, and the length of the trapped column of air increases. As the water cools, the length of the air column decreases.
- Regularly record the temperature of the water and the air column length as the water cools.
- Plot your results on a graph of length against temperature in kelvin. A line of best fit will give a straight line through the origin. This shows that the length of the air column is directly proportional to the temperature in kelvin. The volume of the air column is proportional to its length, so the volume is also proportional to the temperature. This agrees with Charles' Law.

5) These results can be explained using the kinetic model. When the water in the beaker is heated, the trapped air in the capillary tube is heated. The air particles gain kinetic energy and move faster. As the pressure is constant, they move further apart, so the volume of trapped air increases, pushing the drop of sulfuric acid upwards.
6) As the water temperature in the beaker cools, the reverse happens and the volume decreases.

If you Combine All Three Gas Laws you get the Ideal Gas Equation

The ideal gas equation (sometimes called the general gas equation) combines all three of the gas laws. Any of pressure, temperature and volume can change — none are constant. The ideal gas equation can be written in two ways:

Don't forget T is temperature in kelvin.

$$\frac{pV}{T} = \text{constant}$$

$$\frac{p_1 V_1}{T_1} = \frac{p_2 V_2}{T_2}$$

You won't be given this equation in your exam.

Ideal revision equation: marks = pages read × questions answered

Make sure you can sketch the graph for each gas law (and that you know what label goes on each axis).

Q1 A gas has a volume of 5.0 m³ at 250 K. It is heated to 300 K.
Calculate the final volume of the gas. Assume that the mass and pressure are fixed. [3 marks]

Section 4 — Properties of Matter

Revision Questions for Section 4

And you've reached the end of Section 4, woohoo — time to give your old grey matter a workout.
- Try these questions and tick off each one when you get it right.
- When you've done all the questions for a topic and are completely happy with it, tick off the topic.

The Kinetic Model (p.50)

1) For each state of matter, describe the arrangement of the particles.
2) True or false? The particles in a liquid generally have more kinetic energy than the particles in a solid.
3) Describe what happens when you cool down a substance in terms of the kinetic model.
4) What is the value of absolute zero in degrees Celsius?
5) In terms of the kinetic energy of particles, what is the temperature of a substance?

Specific Heat Capacity and Specific Latent Heat (p.51-52)

6) Define specific heat capacity.
7) Give the equation that involves specific heat capacity.
8) When carrying out an experiment to find the specific heat capacity of water, why is an insulated container used to contain the water?
9) If you know the power of a device, how can you calculate the heat energy supplied over a period of time?
10) Define the specific latent heat of a substance.
11) On a graph of temperature against time for heating or cooling a substance, what do the flat horizontal parts of the graph represent?
12) What is the specific latent heat called for a change of state between:
    a) a solid and a liquid?   b) a liquid and a gas?
13) Give the formula involving specific latent heat.

Pressure and Gas Laws (p.53-56)

14) Define pressure and state the equation linking pressure, force and area.
15) Use the kinetic model to explain how gas particles create pressure.
16) What is the relationship between pressure and volume at a constant temperature?
17) Explain Boyle's Law using the kinetic model.
18) What happens to the pressure of a gas in a sealed container of fixed volume when it is heated? Explain why this happens.
19) Describe an experiment you could do to investigate Charles' Law.
20) What are the two ways of writing the ideal gas equation?

Section 4 — Properties of Matter

Wave Properties

Waves transfer energy from one place to another without transferring any matter (stuff). Clever so and so's.

Waves Transfer Energy in the Direction they are Travelling

When waves travel through a medium, the particles of the medium vibrate and transfer energy between each other. BUT overall, the particles stay in the same place.

> For example, if you drop a twig into a calm pool of water, ripples form on, and move across, the water's surface. The ripples don't carry the water (or the twig) away with them though.
>
> Similarly, if you strum a guitar string and create a sound wave, the sound wave travels to your ear (so you can hear it) but it doesn't carry the air away from the guitar — if it did, it would create a vacuum.

1) The amplitude of a wave is the displacement from the rest position to a crest or trough. The bigger the amplitude, the more energy the wave transfers.
2) The wavelength is the length of a full wave (e.g. from crest to crest, or from trough to trough — see graph on the right).
3) Frequency is the number of complete waves passing a certain point per second. Frequency is measured in hertz (Hz). 1 Hz is 1 wave per second.
4) The period of a wave is the number of seconds for one full wave to pass a point.
5) The frequency and period of a wave can be calculated using:

This graph is the same for both transverse and longitudinal waves (see below).

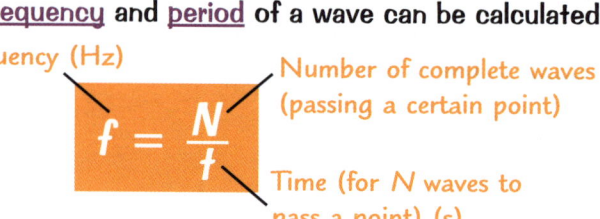

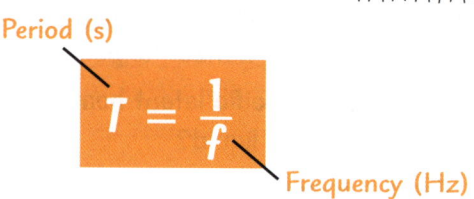

Frequency (Hz)
Number of complete waves (passing a certain point)
$$f = \frac{N}{t}$$
Time (for N waves to pass a point) (s)

Period (s)
$$T = \frac{1}{f}$$
Frequency (Hz)

Transverse Waves Have Sideways Vibrations

In transverse waves, the vibrations are perpendicular (at 90°) to the direction the wave travels. Most waves are transverse, including: 1) All electromagnetic waves, e.g. light (p.61).
2) Ripples in water (see next page).

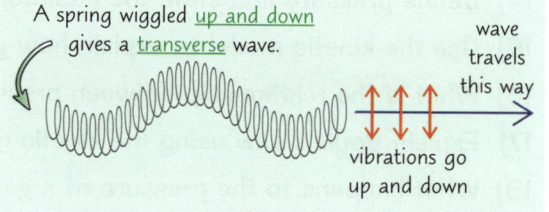

Longitudinal Waves Have Parallel Vibrations

1) In longitudinal waves, the vibrations are parallel to the direction the wave travels.
2) An example of longitudinal waves are sound waves.
3) Longitudinal waves squash up and stretch out the arrangement of particles in the medium they pass through, making compressions (high pressure, lots of particles) and rarefactions (low pressure, fewer particles).

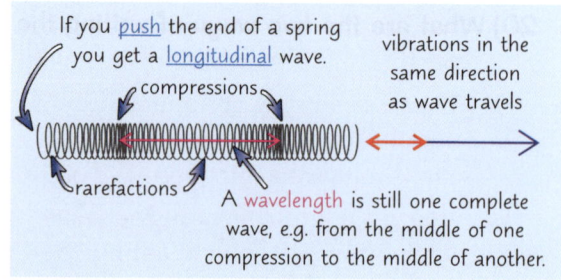

What about Mexican waves...

You won't get far unless you understand these wave basics. Try a question to test your knowledge.

Q1   Give an example of   a) a transverse wave,   b) a longitudinal wave.   [2 marks]

Wave Speed

Time for some wave speed experiments. Microphones and ripple tanks sound fun, just don't mix them together.

You can use Two Equations to Calculate Wave Speed

Wave speed is no different to any other speed — it tells you how quickly a wave moves.
There are two ways to calculate wave speed:

Wave speed (ms⁻¹) $v = \dfrac{d}{t}$ — Distance (m), Time (s)

Wave speed (ms⁻¹) $v = f\lambda$ — Wavelength (m), Frequency (Hz)

EXAMPLE:
A wave in the sea travels 30 m in 20 s. Calculate the speed of the sea wave.
$v = \dfrac{d}{t} = \dfrac{30}{20} = 1.5$ ms⁻¹

Use an Oscilloscope to Measure the Speed of Sound   **PRACTICAL**

By attaching a signal generator to a speaker you can generate sounds with a specific frequency. You can use two microphones and an oscilloscope to find the speed of the sound waves generated.

1) Set up the oscilloscope so the detected waves at each microphone are shown as separate waves.
2) Start with both microphones next to the speaker, then slowly move one away until the two waves are aligned on the display, but have moved exactly one wavelength apart.
3) Measure the distance between the microphones to find one wavelength (λ).
4) You can then use the formula $v = f\lambda$ to find the speed (v) of the sound waves passing through the air — the frequency (f) is whatever you set the signal generator to.
5) The speed of sound in air is around 340 ms⁻¹, so check your results roughly agree with this.

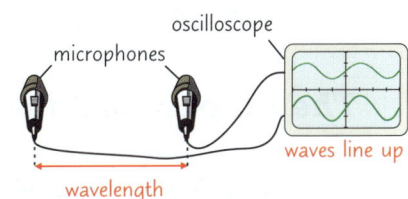

Measure the Speed of Water Ripples Using a Lamp   **PRACTICAL**

1) Using a signal generator attached to the dipper of a ripple tank you can create water waves at a set frequency.
2) Use a lamp to see wave crests on a screen below the tank.
3) The distance between each shadow line is equal to one wavelength. Measure the distance between shadow lines that are 10 wavelengths apart, then divide this distance by 10 to find the value of a single wavelength.
4) If you're struggling to measure the distance, you could take a photo of the shadows and ruler, and find the wavelength from the photo instead.
5) Use $v = f\lambda$ to calculate the wave speed of the water waves — again the frequency is set by the signal generator.

Make sure you dim the lights for this experiment.

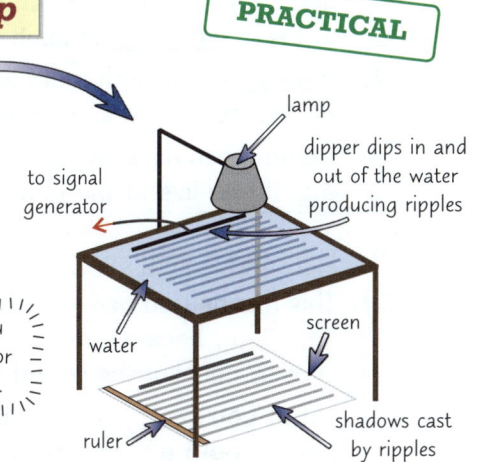

Surf's up, it's time to, like, totally measure some waves...

Once you're confident using those equations, give yourself a high five. Which I suppose is just clapping really...

Q1   A wave has a speed of 0.15 ms⁻¹ and a wavelength of 7.5 cm. Calculate its frequency.   [3 marks]

Diffraction

How much a wave diffracts depends on its wavelength. And how much you learn depends on your brainlength.

Diffraction — Waves Spreading Out

1) All waves spread out ('diffract') at the edges when they pass through a gap or pass around an object.
2) When a wave spreads out, its energy also spreads out. This means its amplitude decreases as it diffracts.
3) When passing through a gap, the amount of diffraction depends on the size of the gap relative to the wavelength of the wave. The narrower the gap, or the longer the wavelength (see below) the more the wave spreads out.
4) A narrow gap is one about the same size as the wavelength of the wave. So whether a gap is classed as narrow depends on the wave. A wavefront diagram can be used to show how much a wave diffracts:

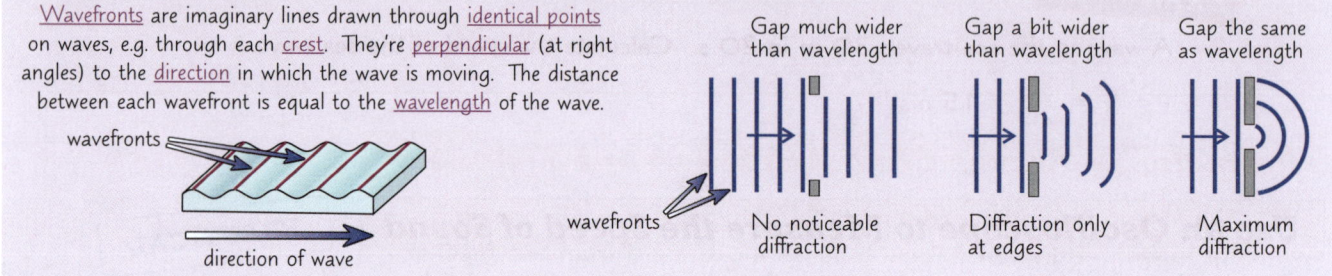

Wavefronts are imaginary lines drawn through identical points on waves, e.g. through each crest. They're perpendicular (at right angles) to the direction in which the wave is moving. The distance between each wavefront is equal to the wavelength of the wave.

5) You get diffraction around the edges of objects too. The shadow is where the wave is blocked. The wider the object compared to the wavelength, the less diffraction it causes, so the shadow is longer.

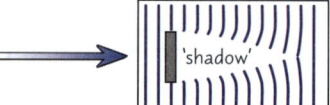

The Amount of Diffraction Depends on the Wavelength

1) Radio waves and microwaves are used in communications (e.g. TV and radio, p.62).
2) Longer wavelength radio waves are able to diffract around corners and any large objects — such as hills, tall buildings etc.
3) So longer wavelength radio waves can travel long distances between the transmitter and receiver without them having to be in the line of sight of each other.
4) Shorter wavelength radio waves and microwaves don't diffract very much, so the transmitters need to be located high up to avoid large objects.
5) Some areas have trouble receiving shorter wavelength radio (and microwave) signals — e.g. if you live at the foot of a mountain you will probably have poor signal strength.

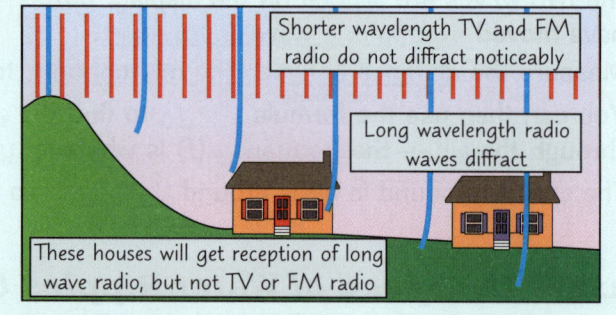

1) Light has a very small wavelength, so it is only diffracted if the gap is really small.
2) This means you can hear someone through an open door even if you can't see them, because the size of the gap and the wavelength of sound are similar, causing the sound wave to diffract and fill the room...
3) ...But you can't see them unless they're in direct line of sight through the door because the gap is about a million times bigger than the wavelength of light, so it won't diffract enough.

Concentrate and don't get diffracted...

All waves can be diffracted. It doesn't matter what type of wave it is — sound, light, water...

Q1 Draw a wavefront diagram to show what happens when a wave passes through a gap with a width the same as its wavelength.

[2 marks]

Electromagnetic Waves and Refraction

You know that light is a wave, but did you know that light's just a small part of the electromagnetic spectrum...

There's a Continuous Spectrum of Electromagnetic Waves

1) Electromagnetic (EM) waves are transverse waves (p.58). They all travel at the same speed through space (a vacuum). This is called the speed of light, and approximately equals 3.00×10^8 ms^{-1}.

2) They are grouped based on their wavelength and frequency — there are seven bands, but the different groups merge to form a continuous spectrum.

EM waves are actually vibrations of electric and magnetic fields.

RADIO WAVES	MICRO WAVES	INFRA RED	VISIBLE LIGHT	ULTRA VIOLET	X-RAYS	GAMMA RAYS
1 m – 10^4 m	10^{-2} m	10^{-5} m	10^{-7} m	10^{-8} m	10^{-10} m	10^{-15} m
10^4 - 10^8 Hz	10^{10} Hz	10^{13} Hz	10^{15} Hz	10^{16} Hz	10^{18} Hz	10^{23} Hz

← Wavelength
← Frequency

Refraction — Waves Changing Speed at a Boundary

1) The higher the density of a material, the slower a wave travels through it. So when a wave crosses a boundary from one medium (material) to another, e.g. from glass to air, it changes speed.

2) The frequency of the wave stays the same when it crosses a boundary, but the wavelength changes.

3) If the wave hits the boundary at an angle, the change in speed (and wavelength) makes the wave bend — this is called refraction. The greater the change in speed, the more it bends.

4) You can use the normal to describe how a wave has been refracted. The normal is an imaginary line that is at right angles to the boundary at the point the light hits it (drawn with a dotted line).

5) If a wave crosses a boundary from a less dense to a more dense medium, the wave will slow down, its wavelength will decrease, and it will bend towards the normal.

6) If a wave crosses a boundary from a more dense to a less dense medium, the wave will speed up, its wavelength will increase, and it will bend away from the normal.

7) If the wave is travelling along the normal it changes speed, but NOT direction.

For light, when we say density we mean optical density — how the material affects the speed of light.

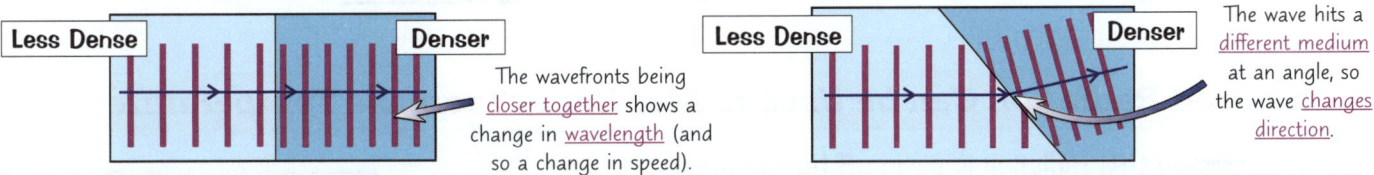

The wavefronts being closer together shows a change in wavelength (and so a change in speed).

The wave hits a different medium at an angle, so the wave changes direction.

A ray is a straight line showing the path a wave travels along. To make a ray diagram for refraction:

1) First, start by drawing the boundary between your two materials and the normal (a line that is at 90° to the boundary).

2) Draw an incident ray that meets the normal at the boundary. The angle between the ray and the normal is the angle of incidence.

3) Now draw the refracted ray on the other side of the boundary. If the second material is denser than the first, the refracted ray bends towards the normal (like on the right). The angle between the refracted ray and the normal (the angle of refraction) is smaller than the angle of incidence. If the second material is less dense, the angle of refraction is larger than the angle of incidence.

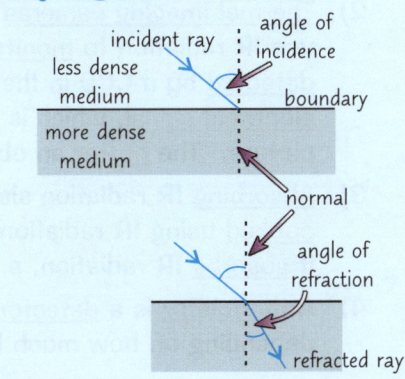

Lights, camera, refraction...

So a wave speeds up going into a less dense medium, and slows down going into a more dense medium. Neat-o.

Q1 Draw a ray diagram for a light ray entering a less dense medium at 40° to the normal. [3 marks]

Sources and Uses of EM Waves

How EM waves behave in materials varies, which means we use different types of EM waves in different ways...

Radio Waves are Used Mainly for Communications

1) We use radio waves to transmit information, like television and radio shows, from one place to another.
2) A radio transmitter is a source of radio waves, and radio waves can be detected by TV and radio aerials and radar dishes.
3) Long-wave radio can be received halfway round the world from where they started, because long wavelengths bend around the curved surface of the Earth (p.60). This makes it possible for radio signals to be received even if the receiver isn't in line of the sight of the transmitter.
4) Short-wave radio signals can, like long-wave, be received at long distances from the transmitter. That's because they are reflected by the Earth's atmosphere.
5) The radio waves used for TV and FM radio transmissions have very short wavelengths. To get reception, you must be in direct sight of the transmitter — the signal doesn't bend or travel far through buildings.
6) Radio waves are also used to observe the universe — radio telescopes on Earth can detect radio signals from outer space (p.30).

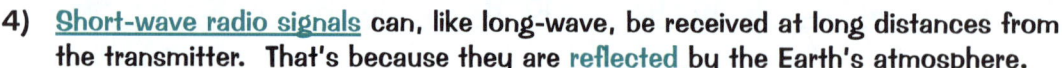

Microwaves are Used for Communications and Cooking

1) Communication to and from satellites (including satellite TV signals and GPS signals) uses microwaves with a wavelength that can pass through the Earth's watery atmosphere. The microwaves are then detected by an aerial.
2) Microwave ovens are a source of microwaves. They emit microwaves of a slightly different wavelength to cook food. These microwaves penetrate up to a few centimetres into the food before being absorbed and transferring energy to water molecules in the food, causing them to heat up. The water molecules then transfer this energy to the rest of the molecules in the food, which quickly cooks the food.

Infrared Radiation Can be Used to Monitor or Increase Temperature

1) Infrared (IR) radiation is given off by all objects. The hotter the object, the more it gives off.
2) Thermal imaging cameras (e.g. night vision cameras) use IR radiation to monitor temperature. The IR is detected by a CCD in the camera and turned into an electrical signal, which is displayed on a screen as a picture. The hotter an object is, the brighter it appears.
3) Absorbing IR radiation also causes objects to get hotter. Food can be cooked using IR radiation — the temperature of the food increases when it absorbs IR radiation, e.g. from a toaster's heating element.
4) A thermistor is a detector of IR radiation — its resistance changes depending on how much IR it receives (p.41).

So many waves — my arms are getting tired...

The next time you're feeling hungry and zap some food in the microwave, think of it as doing revision.

Q1   Give an example of a detector of infrared radiation.   [1 mark]

More Sources and Uses of EM Waves

If you enjoyed the last page, you're in for a real treat. If not, well, you've just got to suck it up.

Visible Light Signals Can Travel Through Optical Fibres

1) Visible light allows us to see things. It's emitted by e.g. light bulbs, the Sun and LEDs (p.41), and it can be detected by e.g. photographic film, the retina in our eyes and LDRs (p.41).
2) Visible light can be used for communication using optical fibres. These carry data over long distances as pulses of light.
3) Optical fibres work by bouncing light off the sides of a very narrow core. The pulse of light enters the core at a certain angle at one end and is reflected again and again until it emerges at the other end.
4) Optical fibres are used for telephone and internet cables. They're also used for medical purposes to see inside the body.

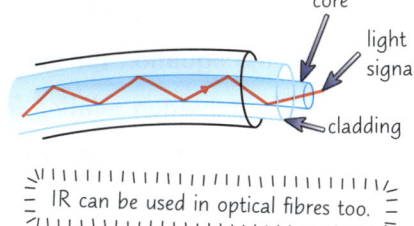
IR can be used in optical fibres too.

Ultraviolet is Used in Fluorescent Lamps

1) The Sun and ultraviolet (UV) lamps are sources of ultraviolet light.
2) UV light can be detected as it causes certain materials to fluoresce. Fluorescence is a property of certain chemicals, where UV radiation is absorbed and then visible light is emitted. That's why fluorescent colours look so bright — they actually emit light.
3) Fluorescent lights work by generating UV radiation which is absorbed and re-emitted as visible light by a layer of phosphor on the inside of the bulb. They're very energy-efficient.
4) Security pens can be used to mark property (e.g. laptops). UV light causes the ink to fluoresce, but the ink is invisible in visible light.
5) UV lamps are also used in tanning salons to give people an artificial suntan.

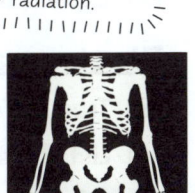
Skin produces a brown pigment in response to UV radiation.

X-rays Let Us See Inside Things

1) X-rays can be produced in X-ray machines by firing very fast electrons at a metal target.
2) X-rays can be used to view the internal structure of objects and materials.
3) Radiographers in hospitals take X-ray images to help doctors diagnose broken bones. X-rays are transmitted by flesh but are absorbed by denser material, like bones or metal.
4) To produce an X-ray image, X-ray radiation is directed through the object or body onto a special type of photographic film. The brighter bits of the image are where fewer X-rays get through, producing a negative image (the plate starts off all white).

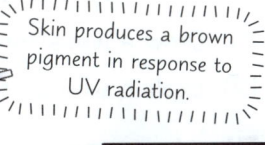

Gamma Rays are Used for Sterilising Things

1) Gamma rays are emitted during the nuclear decay of some radioactive nuclei (p.65). They can be detected using a Geiger-Müller tube and counter (p.66).
2) Gamma rays are used to sterilise medical instruments. If they're absorbed by microbes (e.g. bacteria), they kill them. They also pass through the instruments to reach any microbes hiding in crevices.
3) This is better than trying to boil plastic instruments, which might be damaged by high temperatures.
4) Food can be sterilised in the same way — again killing microbes. This keeps the food fresh for longer, without having to freeze it, cook it or preserve it some other way, and it's perfectly safe to eat.
5) Gamma radiation is also used in cancer treatments (p.68) — radiation is targeted at cancer cells to kill them. Doctors have to be careful to minimise the damage to healthy cells when treating cancer like this.
6) We also use gamma radiation in medical imaging (see p.68).

Don't lie to an X-ray — they can see right through you...

I hate to say it, but go back to page 62 and read all of the sources and uses for EM waves again so you know them.

Q1 Give two uses of gamma rays. [2 marks]

Section 5 — Waves

Revision Questions for Section 5

It's nearly time to wave goodbye to Section 5 — but you know the drill, it's time for some questions first.
- Try these questions and tick off each one when you get it right.
- When you've done all the questions for a topic and are completely happy with it, tick off the topic.

Wave Basics (p.58-59)

1) What is the amplitude, wavelength, frequency and period of a wave?
2) State the equation for the period of a wave, defining any symbols used.
3) Give the equation relating frequency, number of complete waves passing a point, and time.
4) Give the unit for frequency.
5) Describe the difference between transverse and longitudinal waves.
6) Are sound waves transverse or longitudinal?
7) State the equation that can be used to calculate wave speed from frequency and wavelength. Give the units for each quantity in the equation.
8) Give the equation that can be used to calculate wave speed from distance travelled and time.

Diffraction (p.60)

9) What happens to the energy and amplitude of a wave when it is diffracted?
10) Which causes most diffraction: an object much wider than the wavelength of the wave or an object roughly as wide as the wavelength of the wave?
11) Draw a wavefront diagram to show a wave diffracting around an object.
12) Explain why a house at the base of a hill might receive radio signals but not microwave signals.

Electromagnetic Waves and Refraction (p.61-63)

13) True or false? All electromagnetic waves are transverse waves.
14) List the seven bands of the electromagnetic spectrum in order of increasing wavelength.
15) What happens to the speed and wavelength of a wave as it enters a more dense medium?
16) Draw a ray diagram for a light ray entering a less dense medium:
    a) at an angle of incidence of 0°,
    b) at an angle of incidence above 0°.
17) Give one source for each type of EM wave.
18) Give one detector for each type of EM wave.
19) Give one use of each type of EM wave.

Section 5 — Waves

Section 6 — Radiation

Nuclear Radiation

Isotopes and ionisation. They sound similar, but they're totally different, so read this page carefully.

Isotopes are Different Forms of the Same Element

1) All atoms of each element have a set number of protons. The number of protons in an atom is its atomic number.
2) The mass number of an atom is the number of protons plus the number of neutrons in its nucleus.
3) Isotopes of an element are atoms with the same number of protons (the same atomic number) but a different number of neutrons (a different mass number). E.g. $^{18}_{8}O$ is an isotope of oxygen.
4) All elements have different isotopes, but there are usually only one or two stable ones.
5) The other unstable isotopes tend to decay (or disintegrate) into other elements and give out radiation as they try to become more stable. This process is called radioactive decay.

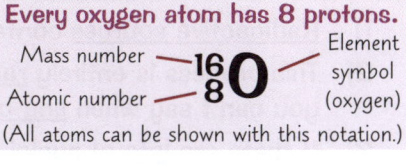

Every oxygen atom has 8 protons.
Mass number — $^{16}_{8}O$ — Element symbol (oxygen)
Atomic number
(All atoms can be shown with this notation.)

Radioactive Isotopes Release Ionising Radiation

1) Atoms are neutral, they have no overall charge. If ionising radiation interacts with an atom it can cause the atom to lose an electron, meaning the atom becomes positively charged. This is called ionisation and the atom is called an ion. The ionising power of radiation tells you how easily it can do this.
2) Radioactive substances spit out one or more types of ionising radiation from their nuclei — the types you need to know are alpha, beta and gamma radiation.

Alpha Particles are Helium Nuclei

1) Alpha decay is when an alpha particle (α) is emitted from the nucleus. An α-particle is two neutrons and two protons (like a helium nucleus).
2) An alpha particle has a mass of 4 atomic units and a charge of +2.
3) They don't penetrate very far into materials and are stopped quickly — they can only travel a few cm in air and are absorbed by a sheet of paper.
4) Because of their size and charge they are strongly ionising.

Alpha radiation is used in smoke detectors — it ionises air particles, causing a current to flow. If there is smoke in the air, it binds to the ions — meaning the current stops and the alarm sounds.

Beta Particles are High-Speed Electrons → e⁻

1) A beta particle (β) is simply a fast-moving electron released by the nucleus when a neutron turns into a proton. Beta particles have virtually no mass and a charge of –1.
2) They are moderately ionising. They penetrate moderately far into materials before colliding and have a range in air of up to a few metres. They are absorbed by a sheet of aluminium (around 5 mm).

Beta emitters are used to test the thickness of sheets of paper (see p.69), as the particles are not immediately absorbed by the material like alpha radiation would be and do not penetrate as far as gamma rays.

Gamma Rays are EM Waves with a Short Wavelength

1) Gamma rays (γ) are waves of high frequency electromagnetic radiation (p.61) released by the nucleus.
2) This means they have no mass and no charge.
3) They penetrate far into materials without being stopped and will travel a long distance through air.
4) This means they are weakly ionising because they tend to pass through rather than collide with atoms. Eventually they hit something and do damage.
5) They can be absorbed by thick sheets of lead or metres of concrete.

Uses of gamma rays are on p.63 and p.68-69.

Ionising radiation — good for getting creases out of your clothes...

Knowing different kinds of radiation and what can absorb them usually bags you a few easy marks in an exam.

Q1 In the medical industry, radiation is directed at medical equipment sealed in packaging. The radiation sterilises the equipment. Explain whether alpha radiation would be suitable for this use. [2 marks]

Activity and Half-Life

How quickly unstable nuclei decay is measured using activity and half-life — two very important terms.

Radioactivity is a Totally Random Process

1) Radioactive sources contain radioactive isotopes that give out radiation from the nuclei of their atoms.
2) This process is entirely random. This means that if you have 1000 unstable nuclei, you can't say when any one of them is going to decay, or which one will decay next.
3) If there are lots of nuclei though, you can predict how many will have decayed in a given time based on the half-life of the source (see below).

Activity of a Source = Disintegrations Per Second

1) The rate at which a source decays is called its ACTIVITY.
2) Activity is measured in becquerels, Bq.
   1 Bq is 1 nuclear disintegration (or decay) per second.
3) A larger radioactive sample will have a higher activity because it contains more radioactive atoms.
4) Activity can be measured with a Geiger-Müller tube, which clicks each time it detects radiation. The tube can be attached to a counter, which displays the number of clicks per second (the count rate).

$$A = \frac{N}{t}$$

Activity (Bq) — A
Number of nuclear disintegrations / counts — N
Time (s) — t

EXAMPLE: A radioactive isotope has 36 nuclear disintegrations in 60 s. Calculate the activity.

$A = N \div t = 36 \div 60 = 0.6$ Bq

The Activity of a Source Decreases Over Time

1) Each time a radioactive nucleus decays, one radioactive nucleus becomes stable. As the unstable nuclei all steadily become stable, the activity as a whole decreases.
2) For some isotopes it takes just a few hours before nearly all the unstable nuclei have decayed, whilst for others it takes millions of years.
3) The problem with trying to measure this time is that the activity never reaches zero, so we have to use the idea of half-life to measure how quickly the activity drops off.

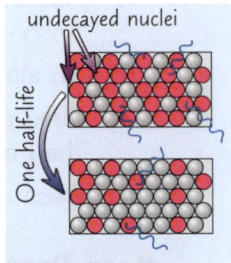

> The half-life is the average time taken for the number of radioactive nuclei in an isotope to halve.

4) A short half-life means the activity falls quickly, because the nuclei are very unstable and rapidly decay. Sources with a short half-life are dangerous because of the high amount of radiation they emit at the start, but they quickly become safe. Half-life can be described as the time taken for the activity to halve.
5) A long half-life means the activity falls more slowly because most of the nuclei don't decay for a long time — the source just sits there, releasing small amounts of radiation for a long time. This can be dangerous because nearby areas are exposed to radiation for (millions of) years.

EXAMPLE: The activity of a radioactive sample is measured as 640 Bq. Two hours later it has fallen to 40 Bq. Find its half-life.

1) Count how many half-lives it took to fall to 40 Bq.

Initial activity:		after 1 half-life:		after 2 half-lives:		after 3 half-lives:		after 4 half-lives:
640	(÷2) →	320	(÷2) →	160	(÷2) →	80	(÷2) →	40

2) Calculate the half-life of the sample. Two hours is four half-lives — so the half-life is 2 hours ÷ 4 = 30 min

My current activity is decreasing over time...

Half-life — the average time for the number of radioactive nuclei or the activity to halve. Simple.

Q1 A radioactive source has a half-life of 60 h and an activity of 480 Bq. Find its activity after 240 h. [3 marks]

Determining Half-Life

Time to put all of that half-life and activity talk into practice with a lovely experiment.

You Can Measure Half-Life Using a Graph

1) If you plot a graph of activity against time (taking into account background radiation, p.70), it will always be shaped like the one to the right.
2) The half-life is found from the graph by finding the time interval on the bottom axis corresponding to a halving of the activity on the vertical axis. Easy.

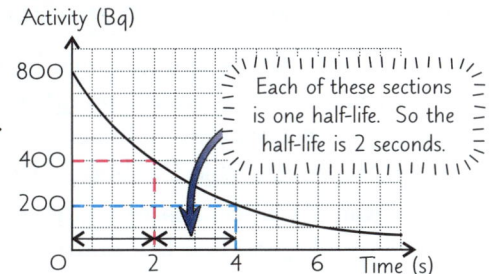

Each of these sections is one half-life. So the half-life is 2 seconds.

EXAMPLE:

The activity of an iodine-131 sample over time is shown in the graph on the right. Calculate the half-life of the sample.

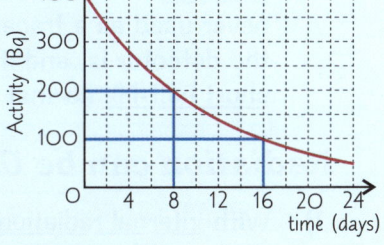

1) First calculate the activity of the sample after 1 half-life. This is just half of the initial activity. $400 \div 2 = 200$ Bq

2) Draw a line from 200 Bq on the y-axis to the curve, and then down to the x-axis. The value on the x-axis gives you the time taken for the activity to halve.   200 Bq gives 8 days on the x-axis

3) You can check that this is right by halving the activity again, and seeing if it has taken another 8 days for it to halve again. $200 \div 2 = 100$ Bq
100 Bq gives 16 days on the x-axis
Half-life = 8 days

You don't have to check your answer but it's a good habit to get into.

You Can do Experiments to Measure Half-Life

You can find the half-life of a radioactive sample by taking measurements of the count rate over time. If you do this experiment in school, you might do it using a radioactive source called a protactinium generator, but it can also be done using computer simulations that represent random decay.
Here's what you need to do:

PRACTICAL

1) Set up the experiment shown. Record the number of counts from the radioactive source over, say, 10 seconds by pointing the Geiger-Müller tube at the source.
2) Calculate the count rate by dividing the number of counts by the time interval.
3) Repeat this measurement at sensible intervals (e.g. every 30 seconds) until the count rate has reduced significantly.
4) Once you've collected your data, take the radioactive source away and measure the background count rate using the Geiger-Müller tube.
5) Subtract the background count rate off each count rate measurement to give the count rate of the sample only — this is called the corrected count rate.
6) Plot a graph of corrected count rate against time. It should look like the graph on the right. You can use this graph to find the half-life in exactly the same way as above.

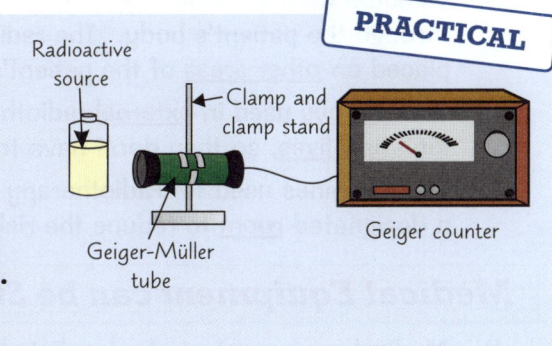

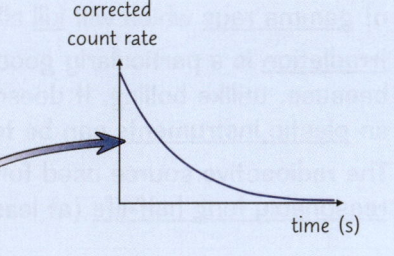

The half-life of a box of chocolates is about five minutes...

The shape of a decay graph is always the same. If you plot one that looks different then something's gone wrong...

Q1 Explain how you would find the corrected count rate of a radioactive sample. [3 marks]

Section 6 — Radiation

Medical Uses of Ionising Radiation

Ionising radiation is very dangerous stuff, but used in the right way it can be incredibly useful.

Radiation Sources can be Used as Medical Tracers

1) Certain radioactive isotopes can be injected into people (or they can just swallow them) and their progress around the body can be followed using an external detector. A computer connected to the detector produces a display showing where the isotope travels in the body. This can help doctors diagnose illnesses.

2) One example is the use of iodine-123, which is absorbed by the thyroid gland just like normal iodine-127, but it gives out radiation which can be detected to indicate whether the thyroid gland is taking in iodine as it should.

3) Isotopes which are taken into the body for use as tracers are usually GAMMA emitters (alpha is never used as a tracer). Gamma radiation is penetrative enough to pass out of the body to where the detector is, and it isn't highly ionising so it doesn't do too much damage. Tracers also need a short half-life so that the radioactivity inside the patient quickly disappears (i.e. within a few hours).

Radiation can be Used Internally or Externally to Treat Cancer

1) With internal radiation therapy, a radioactive material is put inside the body into or near a cancerous tumour. This can be done by e.g. injecting or implanting a small amount of radioactive substance.

2) Alpha emitters are usually injected into the tumour. As alpha particles are strongly ionising, they do lots of damage to the nearby area (the cancerous cells), but the damage to normal tissue surrounding the tumour is limited because they have such a short range. Sources with short half-lives are usually used to limit the patient's exposure to radiation.

3) Beta emitters are often used in implants, placed inside or next to a tumour. Beta radiation is able to penetrate the casing of the implant (unlike alpha particles, which would be stopped) before damaging nearby cancerous cells. As they have a longer range than alpha particles, they can damage healthy cells further away from the cancerous cells. Powerful sources with long half-lives are sometimes used, but these are taken out of the patient after a short time (sometimes after just a few minutes).

4) Tumours can be treated externally using gamma rays aimed at the tumour, as these are able to penetrate through the patient's body. The radiation is carefully focused on the tumour, and sometimes shielding is placed on other areas of the patient's body, but some damage is still done to surrounding healthy cells.

5) The sources used in external radiotherapy treatments should have long half-lives, so they don't have to be replaced often.

6) The machines used for radiotherapy are often surrounded by shielding and kept in a designated room to reduce the risk to staff and patients in the hospital.

Medical Equipment can be Sterilised Using Gamma Rays

1) Medical equipment can be irradiated with a high dose of gamma rays which will kill all microbes.

2) Irradiation is a particularly good method of sterilisation because, unlike boiling, it doesn't involve high temperatures, so plastic instruments can be totally sterilised without being damaged.

3) The radioactive source used for this needs to be a very strong emitter of gamma rays with a reasonably long half-life (at least several months) so that it doesn't need replacing too often.

Gamma radiation — just what the doctor ordered...

It may seem odd to use radiation in medicine, but there you go. Make sure you understand why certain types of radiation are used in each case, and why it's important to consider half-life when choosing a radioactive source.

Q1   Describe how gamma emitters are used as medical tracers.   [2 marks]

Q2   Describe how gamma radiation is used to treat cancerous tumours.   [2 marks]

More Uses of Ionising Radiation

And the uses keep on coming — we use radiation in lots of industrial processes too.

Food can be Sterilised Using Gamma Rays

1) Just like medical equipment (see previous page), food can also be irradiated with a high dose of gamma rays to kill all microbes. This means that the food doesn't go bad as quickly as it otherwise would do.
2) Unlike boiling, this doesn't damage foods like fresh fruit.
3) A source that emits gamma rays must be used. It should have a long half-life so that it doesn't need replacing often.

Radiation is Used in Leak Detection and Thickness Gauges

1) Gamma emitting tracers are also used in industry to detect leaks in underground pipes.
2) The radioactive material is put into one end of the pipe, and a radiation detector outside the pipe tracks the progress of the radioactive material.
3) Beta radiation is used in thickness control in manufacturing. You direct radiation through the stuff being made (e.g. paper), and put a detector on the other side, connected to a control unit. When the amount of detected radiation changes, it means the paper is coming out too thick or too thin, so the control unit adjusts the rollers to give the correct thickness.

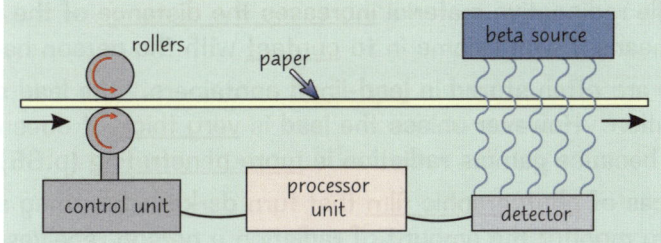

4) The emitter needs to be a beta source, because then the paper will partly block the radiation (see p.65). If it all goes through (or none of it does), then the reading won't change at all as the thickness changes.

Radioactivity can be Used to Date Organic Material

1) The radioactive isotope carbon-14 is used in carbon dating.
2) Living plants take in carbon dioxide, containing the radioactive isotope carbon-14, as part of photosynthesis.
3) When they die, the activity of carbon-14 in the plants starts to fall, with a half-life of around 5730 years.
4) Archaeological finds made from once-living material (like wood) can be dated by finding the current amount of carbon-14 in them, and comparing it to the amount of carbon-14 that would have been in the wood when it was alive.

Carbon dating — for all the single atoms out there...

I've thrown a lot of radiation uses at you over the last two pages. Jot down the key points of each before moving on.

Q1   Give an advantage of radioactive sources used for sterilising food having a long half-life.   [1 mark]

Background Radiation and Risk

Time to find out about the hazards of ionising radiation — it damages living cells when it ionises atoms in them.

Ionising Radiation can be Dangerous

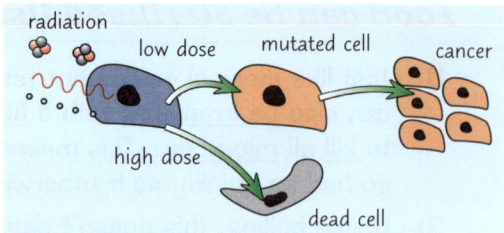

1) Although ionising radiation is very useful it's also very dangerous. It can enter living cells and cause ionisation (see p.65).
2) Low doses of ionising radiation damage living cells by causing mutations in the DNA. This can cause the cells to divide uncontrollably — which is cancer.
3) Higher doses tend to kill cells completely, which causes radiation sickness if a lot of cells are affected.
4) The level of danger depends on the type of radiation.
5) Outside the body, beta and gamma sources are the most dangerous because beta particles and gamma rays can both penetrate the body and get to delicate organs.
6) Alpha particles are the least dangerous outside of the body because they can't penetrate the skin easily.
7) Inside the body, alpha particles are the most dangerous, because they do their damage in a localised area.
8) Beta particles are less damaging inside the body, as radiation is absorbed over a wider area, and some passes out of the body altogether.
9) Gamma rays are the least dangerous inside the body, as they mostly pass straight out of the body.

There are Ways to Protect Against Radiation

1) Gloves or protective clothing should be worn to stop radiation getting onto the skin and shield the body from alpha radiation.
2) Using tongs to handle radioactive material increases the distance of the radiation from the body and also means it won't come in to contact with the person handling it.
3) Radioactive sources are often stored in lead-lined containers. The lead absorbs alpha and beta radiation. However unless the lead is very thick, it doesn't absorb all gamma radiation because gamma radiation is more penetrating (p.65).
4) Film badges are pieces of photographic film that turn darker when they absorb radiation. These can be used to monitor the amount of radiation a person receives.
5) Workers in jobs that have a high risk of exposure to radiation will often have their exposure monitored to make sure that it doesn't go above a certain level (p.72).

Background Radiation Comes From Many Sources

Background radiation is the low-level radiation that's around us all the time.

1) Natural background radiation comes from naturally occurring unstable isotopes in the air, some foods, building materials and some of the rocks under our feet.
2) Natural radiation also comes from space, mostly from the Sun. Luckily, the Earth's atmosphere protects us from most of these 'cosmic rays'. However, the higher up you are, the higher your dose of background radiation from cosmic rays will be.
3) Artificial background radiation is due to human activity. It can come from, e.g. fallout from nuclear explosions, nuclear waste, or medical procedures such as X-rays.
4) Your annual radiation dose varies depending on where you live — the level of background radiation varies according to the type of rock in an area. Your radiation dose will also be higher if you have a job that involves exposure to radiation.

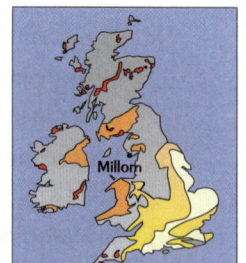

Coloured bits indicate more radiation from rocks

Revision sickness — well yes, it does all get a bit tedious...

If you're working with radioactive sources, read about the safety risks and make experiments as safe as possible.

Q1   Give one effect that ionisation caused by radiation can have on living cells.   [1 mark]

Radiation Dose

Measuring radiation dose is important — it helps to monitor the risks to people who are exposed to radiation.

Absorbed Dose Depends on Energy and Mass

1) When ionising radiation is absorbed, it can cause damage to living cells, see previous page.
2) Absorbed dose is a measure of how much energy is absorbed per unit mass.
3) For a given type of radiation, the bigger the absorbed dose, the more dangerous it is. The more energy that is absorbed, the more likely cells are to be ionised and damaged.
4) If the energy is absorbed by a smaller mass, then it will be more concentrated and so the absorbed dose will be higher.
5) Absorbed dose can be calculated like this:

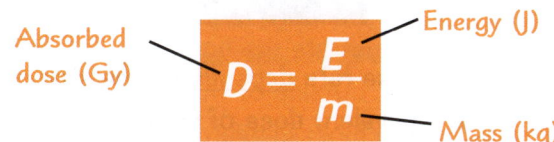

Absorbed dose (Gy) — $D = \dfrac{E}{m}$ — Energy (J), Mass (kg)

6) The unit for absorbed dose is the gray, Gy. 1 Gy = 1 joule per kilogram.

EXAMPLE: A sample of tissue with a mass of 2 kg receives an absorbed dose of 0.05 Gy after being exposed to a radioactive source. Calculate the energy absorbed by the tissue.

1) State the equation above and substitute in the numbers given.
   $D = E \div m$
   $0.05 = E \div 2$
2) Rearrange to find the energy.
   $E = 0.05 \times 2 = 0.1$ J

Equivalent Dose Depends on the Type of Radiation

1) The level of risk from an absorbed dose of radiation depends on how ionising the radiation is.
2) Alpha radiation is much more ionising than beta radiation and gamma radiation, see p.65.
3) The weighting factor is a number that shows the harmful effect of each type of radiation. For alpha radiation it's 20, and for beta and gamma radiation it's 1.
4) Equivalent dose shows how damaging the absorbed dose is depending on the type of radiation.
5) Equivalent dose is measured in sieverts, Sv. You can calculate it using this equation:

Equivalent dose (Sv) — $H = D w_r$ — Weighting factor, Absorbed dose (Gy)

The weighting factors will be given on the data sheet in the exam.

6) This means that if a tissue or organ were to receive equal absorbed doses of alpha and beta radiation, the alpha radiation would be 20 times as harmful.

EXAMPLE: A sample of tissue receives an absorbed dose of 0.02 Gy of alpha radiation and 0.1 Gy of beta radiation. Calculate the total equivalent dose.

1) Use the equation for equivalent dose for the alpha radiation. The weighting factor is 20.
   $H = D \times w_r = 0.02 \times 20 = 0.4$ Sv
2) The weighting factor for beta radiation is 1, so the equivalent dose is the same as the absorbed dose.
   $H = D \times w_r = 0.1 \times 1 = 0.1$ Sv
3) Add together the equivalent doses for both types of radiation to find the total equivalent dose.
   Total $H = 0.4 + 0.1 = 0.5$ Sv

Absorbed knowledge depends on revision and time...

Make sure you understand the difference between absorbed dose and equivalent dose, don't get them mixed up...

Q1 Calculate the absorbed dose when 0.50 J of radiation is absorbed by 250 g of tissue. [3 marks]

Section 6 — Radiation

Comparing Radiation Dose

The radiation dose you receive depends on all sorts, including where you live and what job you do.

Equivalent Dose Rate Depends on the Time of Exposure

1) The risk level of exposure to radiation depends on the time period over which the radiation is absorbed.
2) If you received an equivalent dose of several mSv over a year you would have nothing to worry about, but receiving the same equivalent dose over just a day could be dangerous.
3) The equivalent dose rate takes into account how long the exposure to the equivalent dose lasted.

$$\dot{H} = \frac{H}{t}$$

- Equivalent dose rate (Sv per unit time)
- Equivalent dose (Sv)
- Time (s, minutes, hours etc)

4) The best unit to use for equivalent dose rate depends on the size of the dose and the time period.
5) For example, if you measured an equivalent dose of several millisieverts over a year, the units you would probably be best using would be mSv year^{-1} — if you used kSv s^{-1} the number would be really, really tiny.
6) Try to pick sensible units depending on the size of the equivalent dose and the time period.

There are Limits on Radiation Dose

1) Everyone receives doses of radiation due to natural and artificial sources of background radiation (p.70).
2) The size of these varies according to factors such as the rock type in the area where you live.
3) You also receive a dose of radiation from activities such as having an X-ray, or travelling by plane (because the dose from cosmic rays increases with altitude, p.70).
4) Some jobs will increase the dose you receive, like if you work in a nuclear power station or as an aeroplane pilot.
5) Here are some examples of average equivalent doses in the UK from different types of background radiation, and from activities that would expose someone to radiation.

Background radiation sources	Equivalent dose (mSv)
Annual radon exposure	1.3
Annual cosmic ray exposure	0.3
Annual medical exposure	0.4

Activities that expose you to radiation	Equivalent dose (mSv)
Chest X-ray	0.014
CT head scan	1.4
Transatlantic flight	0.08

Transatlantic means across the Atlantic Ocean (e.g. from the UK to the USA).

6) Effective dose is used to measure the overall long-term risks of a certain exposure. It takes into account the type of tissue or organ that absorbs the radiation (some types of tissue or organ are more likely to be damaged by radiation than other types).
7) You need to learn these three effective equivalent radiation doses below for the exam:

- Average annual background radiation in the UK: 2.2 mSv
- Annual effective dose limit for one member of the public: 1 mSv
- Annual effective dose limit for a radiation worker: 20 mSv

Z z z z z — more like radiation doze...

Learn those three radiation doses in the blue box. It's an easy mark in the exam if you remember them properly.

Q1 A radiation worker receives an average equivalent dose of 0.08 mSv a day. After how many days will the worker reach the annual effective dose limit for a radiation worker? [3 marks]

Nuclear Fission

It's amazing how much energy there is trapped in a little atom. This energy is released by nuclear fission.

Nuclear Fission — the Splitting Up of Big Atomic Nuclei

Nuclear fission is a type of nuclear reaction that is used to release energy from uranium (or plutonium) atoms, e.g. in a nuclear reactor. Huge amounts of energy can be released this way by using a chain reaction...

The Chain Reaction:

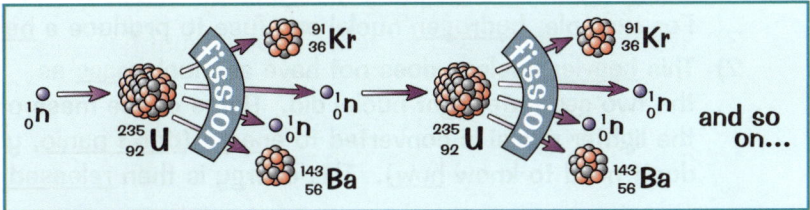

1) A slow-moving neutron is fired at a large, unstable nucleus — often uranium-235. The neutron is absorbed by the nucleus — this makes the atom more unstable and causes it to split.

2) When the U-235 atom splits it forms two new lighter elements ('daughter nuclei') and energy is released.

3) There are lots of different pairs of atoms that uranium can split into, e.g. krypton-91 and barium-143, but all these new nuclei are radioactive.

4) Each time a uranium atom splits up, it also spits out two or three neutrons, which can hit other uranium nuclei, causing them to split also, and so on and so on. This is a chain reaction.

Chain Reactions in Reactors Must be Carefully Controlled

1) The neutrons released by fission reactions in a nuclear reactor have a lot of energy.

2) These neutrons will only cause other nuclear fissions (and cause a chain reaction) if they are moving slowly enough to be captured by the uranium nuclei in the fuel rods. These slow-moving neutrons are called thermal neutrons.

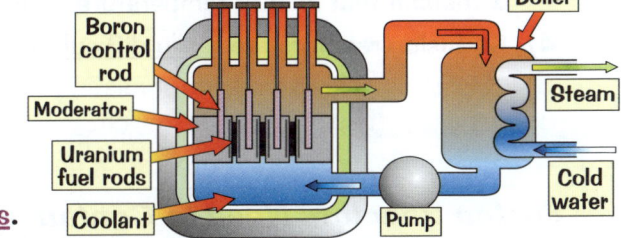

3) In order for a chain reaction to happen, the uranium fuel rods are placed in a moderator (for example, graphite) to slow down the fast-moving neutrons.

4) Control rods, often made of boron, limit the rate of fission by absorbing excess neutrons. They are placed in between the fuel rods and are raised and lowered into the reactor to control the chain reaction.

5) This creates a steady rate of nuclear fission, where one new neutron produces another fission.

6) If the chain reaction in a nuclear reactor is left to continue unchecked, large amounts of energy are released in a very short time. Many new fissions will follow each fission, causing a runaway reaction which could lead to an explosion.

Nuclear Power Stations use energy from Fission

1) Nuclear power stations are powered by nuclear reactors that create controlled chain reactions.

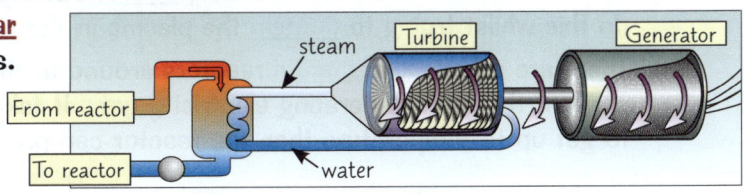

2) The energy released by fission is converted to heat energy. This heat energy heats up the cold water passing through the boiler, causing the water to boil and turn to steam.

3) The steam turns a turbine, which itself turns a generator. When the generator turns it produces electricity.

Revise nuclear power — full steam ahead...

Nuclear reactors are carefully-designed to release energy safely, but they still have issues.

Q1   Draw a diagram showing how fission can lead to a chain reaction.   [3 marks]

Nuclear Fusion

Loads of energy's released either when you break apart really big nuclei or join together really small nuclei. You can't do much with the ones in the middle, I'm afraid. But at least that's one less thing to learn...

Nuclear Fusion — Joining Small Nuclei

1) Nuclear fusion is the opposite of nuclear fission. In nuclear fusion, two light nuclei collide at high speed and join (fuse) to create a larger, heavier nucleus. For example, hydrogen nuclei can fuse to produce a helium nucleus.
2) This heavier nucleus does not have as much mass as the two separate, light nuclei did. Some of the mass of the lighter nuclei is converted to energy (don't panic, you don't need to know how). This energy is then released as radiation.

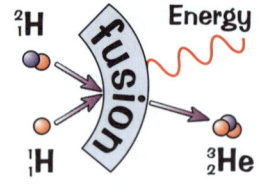

It's Hard to make Fusion Happen

1) The big problem is that fusion only happens at really high pressures and temperatures (about 10 000 000 °C).
2) This is because the positively charged nuclei have to get very close to fuse, so the strong force due to electrostatic repulsion (p.37) has to be overcome.
3) It's really hard to create the right conditions for fusion. No material can withstand that kind of temperature — it would just be vaporised.
4) So fusion reactors are really difficult and expensive to build.

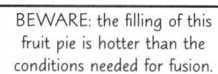

BEWARE: the filling of this fruit pie is hotter than the conditions needed for fusion.

Fusion Reactors Need to Contain a Plasma

1) When atoms are heated to high enough temperatures they form a new state called a plasma.
2) Plasma is extremely hard to contain because it is too hot to come into contact with any material.
3) A fusion reactor heats hydrogen to temperatures so high that it becomes a plasma.
4) One approach to containing this very hot hydrogen plasma is to use very strong magnetic fields, but this method is currently still being tested.
5) Fusion reactors aim to work just like most power stations do. Nuclear fusion releases a lot of heat which would be used to turn water into steam to power a steam turbine (see previous page).
6) Fuel would need to be continuously added, but it's very difficult to do this whilst trying to contain the plasma in the reactor.
7) There are a few experimental reactors around at the moment, but none of them are generating electricity yet. It takes more power to get up to temperature than the reactor can produce.

Pity they can't release energy by confusion...

Thankfully you don't need to know the complicated processes behind fusion, you just need to have an idea of the main steps it involves. Remember, fusion is combining small nuclei for energy. Nowt else to it. Well...

Q1   Give one reason why nuclear fusion is difficult to recreate on Earth.   [1 mark]

Section 6 — Radiation

Revision Questions for Section 6

Section 6 has nearly come to an end — but first, a little treat in the form of some lovely revision questions.
- Try these questions and tick off each one when you get it right.
- When you've done all the questions for a topic and are completely happy with it, tick off the topic.

Nuclear Decay and Half-Life (p.65-67)

1) What is meant by 'ionisation'?
2) What is radioactive decay?
3) For the three types of ionising radiation, give: a) their relative ionising power, b) their range in air.
4) What are the masses and charges of the three types of radiation?
5) What is the equation for the activity of a radioactive source? What are its units?
6) Define half-life.
7) Sketch a graph of the activity of a radioactive source against time.
8) Explain how you would find the half-life of a source, given a graph of its activity against time.
9) What is corrected count rate?
10) Describe an experiment that you could do to find the half-life of a radioactive source.

Uses of Ionising Radiation (p.68-69)

11) Explain why an alpha emitter wouldn't be used as a medical tracer.
12) Should a radioactive source with a long or short half-life be used as a medical tracer?
13) Why is it better to use gamma rays rather than boiling to sterilise plastic medical equipment?
14) Explain how radiation can be used to detect leaks in pipes.
15) Explain why alpha radiation could not be used to check the thickness of metal sheets.

Radiation Dose (p.70-72)

16) Explain how exposure to radiation can lead to cancer.
17) Which types of radiation are the most dangerous outside of the body? Explain why.
18) Why are radiation sources stored in lead-lined containers?
19) Give two examples of how people can protect themselves when working with radiation.
20) Give an example of a natural and an artificial source of background radiation.
21) State the equation for absorbed dose.
22) What are the units for absorbed dose?
23) What is the difference between absorbed dose and equivalent dose?
24) State the value for the average annual background radiation effective dose in the UK.

Fission and Fusion (p.73-74)

25) Briefly describe how a fission chain reaction occurs.
26) Explain the function of control rods in a fission reactor.
27) Describe how nuclear fuel is used in a fission power station to generate electricity.
28) State the conditions needed to create a fusion reaction.
29) Why is plasma hard to contain in a fusion reactor?
30) Give an example of how scientists are currently trying to contain plasma in a fusion reactor.

PRACTICAL Apparatus and Techniques

Experiments are covered throughout this book. This section covers some of the practical skills you'll need to know about for these experiments. First up, using apparatus to take measurements...

Mass Should Be Measured Using a Balance

1) For a solid, set the balance to zero and then place your object onto the scale and read off the mass.
2) If you're measuring the mass of a liquid, start by putting an empty container onto the balance. Next, reset the balance to zero.
3) Then just pour your liquid into the container and record the mass displayed. Easy.

Measure Most Lengths with a Ruler

1) In most cases a bog-standard centimetre ruler can be used to measure length.
2) It depends on what you're measuring though — metre rulers or long measuring tapes are handy for large distances. For even longer distances, say for finding someone's average walking speed, you'll want to measure their speed over many metres, so you might use a rolling tape measure (one of those clicky wheel things). They're not as accurate as using a ruler, but they give a good estimate of a longer distance.

When using a ruler, you should always make sure the ruler is parallel to what you want to measure.

Use Division for Tricky Measurements

1) If you're dealing with something where it's tricky to measure just one accurately, you can measure several and divide by how many you've measured to find the value of one.
2) For example, for the wavelength of water ripples (p.59), you can measure the length of e.g. ten of them and then divide by this number to find the length of one.

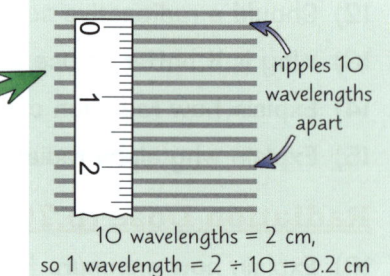

ripples 10 wavelengths apart

10 wavelengths = 2 cm, so 1 wavelength = 2 ÷ 10 = 0.2 cm

Beware of Parallax

1) When measuring lengths, make sure the ruler and the object are always at eye level when you take a reading. This stops parallax affecting your results. E.g. when doing the experiment to verify Charles's Law (p.56), make sure you're at eye level with the droplet of sulfuric acid in the capillary tube.
2) Parallax is where a measurement appears to change based on where you're looking from. The blue line in the diagram shows the real position of the bottom of the droplet relative to the ruler. If the eye isn't level with this line, the droplet appears lower or higher than it really is.

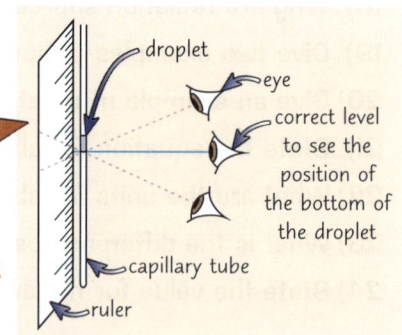

Measure Temperature Accurately with a Thermometer

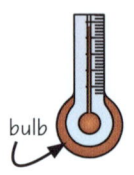

1) Make sure the bulb of your thermometer is completely submerged in any substance you're measuring.
2) Wait for the temperature to stabilise before you take your initial reading. For example, in the practical on page 52, after fully placing the thermometer bulb in the crushed ice, you should wait for the height of the mercury to stop falling before taking the first temperature reading.
3) Again, read your measurement off the scale on a thermometer at eye level.

When you're reading off a scale, use the value of the nearest mark on the scale (the nearest graduation).

Apparatus and Techniques   PRACTICAL

You May Have to Measure the Time Taken for a Change

1) To measure time intervals longer than about 5 seconds, you should use a stopwatch — they're more accurate than regular watches.
2) For shorter time intervals, you could use a light gate instead (p.17). This reduces any large errors in your experiment caused by your reaction time.
3) A video with a known frame rate can also be used to measure the time taken for something to happen — see p.17 for an example of how this is done.

Measure Gas Volumes with a Gas Syringe...

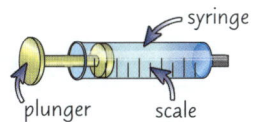

1) Gas syringes are often used to measure volumes of gases. They have scales marked on them like measuring cylinders. You need to know how to use one to verify Boyle's Law (see p.54).
2) Gas syringes come in a range of sizes. Make sure you choose one that's the right size for the measurement you want to make. It's no good using a huge 1 dm^3 syringe to measure 2 cm^3 of gas — the graduations (markings of the scale) will be too big and you'll end up with massive errors. It'd be much better to use one that measures up to 10 cm^3.

...And Gas Pressures with a Pressure Gauge

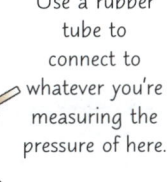

Use a rubber tube to connect to whatever you're measuring the pressure of here.

1) You need to use a pressure gauge (sometimes called a Bourdon gauge) to verify Boyle's Law (p.54) and Gay-Lussac's Law (p.55).
2) If the pressure gauge reads 0 when it isn't connected to anything, this means that when you connect it to something, e.g. a syringe, the pressure gauge is actually measuring the difference between the atmospheric pressure and the pressure of the gas in the syringe.
3) If you want to know the actual gas pressure, you need to add on atmospheric pressure (1 × 10^5 Pa) to your pressure readings.
4) You can use a pressure sensor connected to a data logger or computer to measure pressure too.

Be Careful When You Do Experiments

1) There are always hazards in any experiment, so before you start an experiment you should read and follow any safety precautions to do with your method or the apparatus you're using.
2) Stop equipment falling by using clamp stands. Also, make sure masses are of a sensible size so they don't break the equipment they're used with.
3) When heating something, make sure it's cool before moving it (or wear insulated gloves). If you use an immersion heater to heat a liquid, always let it dry out in air, just in case any liquid has leaked inside it.
4) When working with electronics, make sure you use a low enough voltage and current to prevent wires overheating (and potentially melting) and avoid damage to components, like blowing a filament bulb.
5) You also need to be aware of general safety in the lab — handle glassware carefully so it doesn't break, don't stick your fingers in sockets and avoid touching frayed wires. That kind of thing.

Experimentus apparatus...

Wizardry won't help you here, unfortunately. Most of this should be familiar to you, but make sure you get your head down and know these techniques inside out — you never know, you might be asked about them in the exam.

Performing Experiments

PRACTICAL: Working with Electronics

There are a few experiments that use circuits that will pop up time and time again in your exam. You need to be able to understand and interpret circuit diagrams and know how to measure p.d. and current in circuits.

You Have to Interpret Circuit Diagrams

1) Before you get cracking on an experiment involving any kind of electrical devices, you have to plan and build your circuit using a circuit diagram.
2) Make sure you know all of the circuit symbols on page 38 so you're not stumped before you've even started.

There Are a Couple of Ways to Measure Potential Difference and Current

Voltmeters Measure Potential Difference

1) If you're using an analogue voltmeter, choose the voltmeter with the most appropriate unit (e.g. V or mV). If you're using a digital voltmeter, you'll most likely be able to switch between them.
2) Connect the voltmeter in parallel (p.44) across the component you want to test. The wires that come with a voltmeter are usually red (positive) and black (negative). These go into the red and black coloured ports on the voltmeter. Funnily enough.
3) Then simply read the potential difference from the scale (or from the screen if it's digital).

Ammeters Measure Current

1) Just like with voltmeters, choose the ammeter with the most appropriate unit.
2) Connect the ammeter in series (p.43) with the component you want to test, making sure they're both on the same branch. Again, they usually have red and black ports to show you where to connect your wires.
3) Read off the current shown on the scale or by the screen.

Turn your circuit off between readings to prevent wires overheating and affecting your results (p.39).

Multimeters Measure Both

1) Instead of having a separate ammeter and voltmeter, many circuits use multimeters. These are devices that measure a range of properties — usually potential difference, current and resistance.
2) If you want to find potential difference, make sure the positive wire is plugged into the port that has a 'V' (for volts).
3) To find the current, use the port labelled 'A' or 'mA' (for amps).
4) The dial on the multimeter should then be turned to the relevant section, e.g. to 'A' to measure current in amps. The screen will display the value you're measuring.

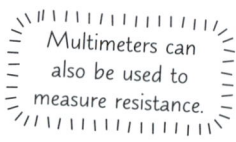

Multimeters can also be used to measure resistance.

My circuit building skills are unparalleled...

Well, that's it folks. Crack open the chocolate bar of victory and know you've earned it. Only the tiny little detail of your actual exam to go... ahem. Good luck — I've got my fingers, toes and eyes crossed for you.

Performing Experiments

Answers

Section 1 — Dynamics

p.13 — Scalars and Vectors
Q1 Scalar quantities only have a size whereas vector quantities also have a direction *[1 mark]*.

p.14 — Resultant Vectors
Q1

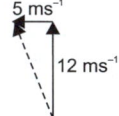

[1 mark for a correct scale drawing]
OR
$R^2 = 12^2 + 5^2$
    $= 169$
$R = \sqrt{169} = 13$ ms^{-1}
[1 mark for correct method]
Resultant velocity = 13 ms^{-1} *[1 mark]*

p.15 — Speed and Velocity
Q1 a) 1.0 ms^{-1} *[1 mark]*
b) $d = \bar{v} t$ *[1 mark]*
    $t = 10 + 8 = 18$ s
    $22 = \bar{v} \times 18$
    so $\bar{v} = 22 \div 18$ *[1 mark]*
        = 1.2 ms^{-1} (2 s.f.) *[1 mark]*

p.16 — Acceleration
Q1 $a = \frac{v-u}{t}$ *[1 mark]*
    $9.8 = \frac{14.7 - 0}{t}$ so $t = \frac{14.7 - 0}{9.8}$ *[1 mark]*
            = 1.5 s *[1 mark]*

p.17 — Measuring Motion
Q1 Use the light gates to time how long it takes the object to travel between the two light gates *[1 mark]*. Measure the distance between the two light gates *[1 mark]*. To find the speed, divide the distance by the time taken for the object to travel between the two light gates *[1 mark]*.

p.18 — Velocity-Time Graphs
Q1 E.g.

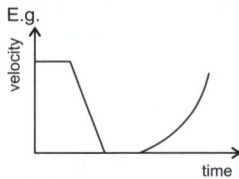

[1 mark for line which is initially horizontal, then becomes a straight line with a negative gradient, continuing until it meets the time axis, 1 mark for showing the line then continuing horizontally along the time axis, and 1 mark for then showing the line curving upwards.]

p.19 — Forces
Q1 E.g.

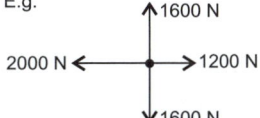

[2 marks for all forces correctly drawn, otherwise 1 mark for three forces correctly drawn — weight and reaction force arrows should be the same length, the arrow for the driving force should be longer than the weight arrow and the arrow for the resistive force should be shorter than the weight arrow.]

p.20 — Newton's First and Second Laws
Q1 $F = ma$ *[1 mark]*
    $= 26\,000 \times 1.5$ *[1 mark]*
    $= 39\,000$ N *[1 mark]*

p.21 — Newton's Third Law
Q1 a) If object A exerts a force on object B, then object B exerts an equal and opposite force on object A *[1 mark]*.
b) The rocket exerts a backwards force on the hot gases from the burning fuel *[1 mark]* and the hot gases exert and equal but opposite forwards force on the rocket *[1 mark]*. If the forwards force exceeds any backwards forces then the rocket will accelerate forwards *[1 mark]*.

p.22 — Weight, Mass and Gravity
Q1 a) $W = mg$ *[1 mark]*
    $= 5 \times 9.8$ *[1 mark]*
    $= 49$ N *[1 mark]*
b) $W = mg$
    $= 5 \times 1.6$ *[1 mark]*
    $= 8$ N *[1 mark]*

p.23 — Terminal Velocity
Q1 As the ball falls the force due to friction/air resistance/drag increases as the object speeds up *[1 mark]*. Eventually the force due to friction/air resistance/drag equals the force of gravity/weight *[1 mark]*. The forces are balanced so the object stops accelerating *[1 mark]*.

p.24 — Energy and Work Done
Q1 20 cm = 0.2 m
    $W = Fd$ *[1 mark]* $= 20 \times 0.2$ *[1 mark]*
            $= 4$ J *[1 mark]*

p.25 — Kinetic and Potential Energy
Q1 The change in height is 5.0 m. So the energy transferred from gravitational potential energy is:
$E_p = mgh$ *[1 mark]*
    $= 2.0 \times 9.8 \times 5.0$ *[1 mark]*
    $= 98$ J
This energy is transferred to kinetic energy so $E_k = 98$ J *[1 mark]*

p.26 — Projectile Motion
Q1 $v_h = s \div t$ *[1 mark]*
    $10 = s \div 4$ so $s = 10 \times 4$ *[1 mark]*
                $= 40$ m *[1 mark]*

p.27 — More Projectile Motion and Satellites
Q1 E.g.

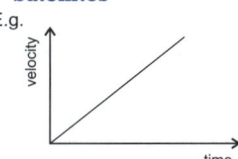

[1 mark for line which starts at the origin, 1 mark for a straight line with a positive gradient]

Section 2 — Space

p.29 — Our Solar System, Our Galaxy and the Universe
Q1 The Milky Way *[1 mark]*
Q2 Convert the time taken for the light to travel to seconds:
$4.2 \times 60 \times 60 \times 24 \times 365.25 = 1.325... \times 10^8$ s
$d = vt$ *[1 mark]*
    $= 3 \times 10^8 \times 1.325... \times 10^8$ *[1 mark]*
    $= 3.976... \times 10^{16}$
    $= 4.0 \times 10^{16}$ m (to 2 s.f.) *[1 mark]*

p.30 — Origin of the Universe
Q1 14 billion years *[1 mark]*

p.31 — Observing the Universe
Q1 A *[1 mark]* and C *[1 mark]*

p.32 — Satellites
Q1 The orbital period will decrease *[1 mark]*.

p.33 — Challenges and Risks of Space Travel
Q1 Astronauts receive a higher level of radiation from cosmic rays because there is no atmosphere to absorb the cosmic rays *[1 mark]*. Cosmic rays are ionising radiation which can damage cells in the body (leading to cancer) *[1 mark]*.

p.34 — More Challenges and Risks of Space Travel
Q1 E.g. use an ion drive *[1 mark]* to reach high speeds without using much fuel *[1 mark]* / accelerate the spacecraft using the gravitational field *[1 mark]* of a fast moving planet/moon/asteroid *[1 mark]*.
This is known as a gravitational catapult/slingshot.

p.35 — Mechanics of Space Travel
Q1 The thrusters exert a force on the hot gases, pushing them backwards out of the rocket *[1 mark]*. These hot gases exert an equal and opposite force on the thrusters, pushing the rocket forwards *[1 mark]*.

Section 3 — Electricity

p.37 — Charge and Electric Fields
Q1 A negatively charged particle would move towards the positive point charge *[1 mark]*.

p.38 — Electrical Current and Circuit Symbols
Q1 $Q = It$ *[1 mark]*
    $28\,000 = 8.0 \times t$
    so $t = 28\,800 \div 8.0$ *[1 mark]*
        $= 3600$ s (= 1 hour) *[1 mark]*

p.39 — Potential Difference and Resistance
Q1 $V = I \times R$ *[1 mark]*
    $8.0 = 4.0 \times R$ so $R = 8.0 \div 4.0$ *[1 mark]*
                    $= 2.0$ Ω *[1 mark]*

p.40 — Investigating Components
Q1

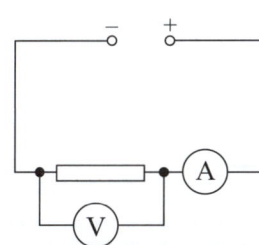

[1 mark for a complete circuit with a variable d.c. power supply in series with a resistor with correct circuit symbols for all components, 1 mark for a voltmeter connected across the resistor and an ammeter connected in series with the resistor.]

p.41 — Circuit Devices
Q1 a) E.g. automatic night lights — a light automatically turns on when it gets dark *[1 mark]*.
b) E.g. thermostats — the heating automatically turns on/off at a certain temperature *[1 mark]*.

p.42 — More Circuit Devices
Q1 Loudspeaker *[1 mark]*

p.43 — Series Circuits
Q1 $V = 12 + 12 = 24$ V *[1 mark]*
    $R = 2 + 3 + 7 = 12$ Ω *[1 mark]*
    $V = I \times R$ *[1 mark]*
    $24 = I \times 12$ so $I = 24 \div 12$
                    $= 2$ A *[1 mark]*

p.44 — Parallel Circuits
Q1 The current through the circuit increases *[1 mark]* and the total resistance of the circuit decreases to less than the resistance of the smallest resistor *[1 mark]*.

p.45 — Potential Dividers
Q1 $V_2 = (\frac{R_2}{R_1 + R_2}) V_s$ *[1 mark]*
    $= (\frac{6}{12 + 6}) \times 12$ *[1 mark]* $= 4$ V *[1 mark]*

Answers

p.46 — Transistors
Q1 As the temperature of the oven hob increases, the resistance of the thermistor decreases *[1 mark]*. The potential difference across the thermistor decreases and the potential difference across the variable resistor increases *[1 mark]*. When the potential difference across the variable resistor increases above a certain value (corresponding to 40 °C), the npn / bipolar transistor switches on the LED *[1 mark]*.

p.47 — Mains Electricity
Q1 In an alternating current (a.c.) supply, the current is constantly changing direction *[1 mark]*. In a direct current (d.c.) supply, the current always travels in the same direction *[1 mark]*.

p.48 — Power
Q1 $P = V^2 \div R$ *[1 mark]*
$55 = (230 \times 230) \div R$
so $R = (230 \times 230) \div 55$ *[1 mark]*
$= 961.818... = 960\ \Omega$ (to 2 s.f.) *[1 mark]*

Section 4 — Properties of Matter

p.50 — The Kinetic Model and Temperature
Q1 $78 + 273 = 351$ K *[1 mark]*

p.51 — Specific Heat Capacity
Q1 $E_h = cm\Delta T$ *[1 mark]*
$1680 = 0.20 \times 420 \times \Delta T$
so $\Delta T = 1680 \div (420 \times 0.20)$ *[1 mark]*
$= 20$ °C (or 20 K) *[1 mark]*

p.52 — Specific Latent Heat
Q1 E.g.

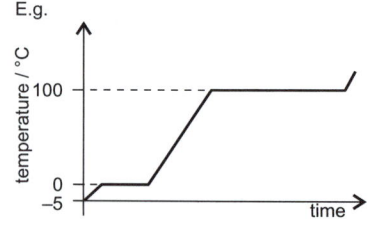

[1 mark for showing the line as flat at 0 °C, 1 mark for showing the line as flat at 100 °C, 1 mark for drawing the line with a positive gradient, for temperatures below 0 °C, between 0 and 100 °C, and above 100 °C.]

p.53 — Pressure
Q1 $p = F \div A$ *[1 mark]*
$A = 0.20 \times 0.12 = 0.024$ m²
$p = 6.0 \div 0.024$ *[1 mark]*
$= 250$ Pa *[1 mark]*

Q2 $p = F \div A$ *[1 mark]*
$p = 300 \div (20 \times 10^{-4})$ *[1 mark]*
$= 150\,000$ Pa *[1 mark]*

p.54 — Gas Laws — Boyle's Law
Q1 E.g. connect an airtight syringe with a scale on it to a pressure gauge *[1 mark]*. Use the plunger on the syringe to vary the volume whilst taking measurements of the volume and pressure at intervals *[1 mark]*. Plot a graph of p against $1 \div V$. The graph should give a straight line through the origin which verifies Boyle's Law *[1 mark]*.

p.55 — Gas Laws — Gay-Lussac's Law
Q1 $\dfrac{p_1}{T_1} = \dfrac{p_2}{T_2}$ *[1 mark]*
$\dfrac{25\,000}{350} = \dfrac{55\,000}{T_2}$
so $T_2 = \dfrac{350 \times 55\,000}{25\,000}$ *[1 mark]*
$= 770$ K *[1 mark]*
$770 - 350 = 420$ K *[1 mark]*

p.56 — Gas Laws — Charles' Law and The Ideal Law
Q1 $\dfrac{V_1}{T_1} = \dfrac{V_2}{T_2}$ *[1 mark]*
$\dfrac{5.0}{250} = \dfrac{V_2}{300}$ so $V_2 = \dfrac{5.0 \times 300}{250}$ *[1 mark]*
$= 6.0$ m³ *[1 mark]*

Section 5 — Waves

p.58 — Wave Properties
Q1 a) E.g. electromagnetic waves / water waves *[1 mark]*
b) E.g. sound waves *[1 mark]*

p.59 — Wave Speed
Q1 $7.5 \div 100 = 0.075$ m
$v = f\lambda$ *[1 mark]*
$0.15 = f \times 0.075$ so $f = 0.15 \div 0.075$ *[1 mark]*
$= 2.0$ Hz *[1 mark]*

p.60 — Diffraction
Q1 E.g.

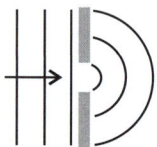

[1 mark for the same distance between each wave front, 1 mark for semicircular waves after passing through the gap]

p.61 — Electromagnetic Waves and Refraction
Q1 E.g.

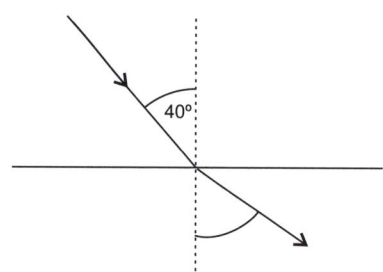

[1 mark for a correct diagram showing rays and the normal, 1 mark for an angle of incidence of 40°, 1 mark for an angle of refraction greater than 40°]

p.62 — Sources and Uses of EM Waves
Q1 E.g. CCD / thermistor *[1 mark]*

p.63 — More Sources and Uses of EM Waves
Q1 Any two from: e.g. sterilising medical equipment / sterilising food / cancer treatment / medical imaging *[2 marks]*.

Section 6 — Radiation

p.65 — Nuclear Radiation
Q1 E.g. Alpha would not be suitable because it is stopped by a few cm of air or a sheet of paper *[1 mark]*. It would not be able to pass through the packaging to sterilise the equipment *[1 mark]*.

p.66 — Activity and Half-Life
Q1 The number of half-lives in 240 hours is $240 \div 60 = 4$ half-lives *[1 mark]*
Initial count = 480
after 1 half-life = $480 \div 2 = 240$
[1 mark for evidence of halving]
after 2 half-lives = $240 \div 2 = 120$
after 3 half-lives = $120 \div 2 = 60$
after 4 half-lives = $60 \div 2 = 30$ Bq *[1 mark]*

p.67 — Determining Half-Life
Q1 E.g. Use a Geiger-Müller counter to measure the count rate of the radioactive substance *[1 mark]*. Measure the background count rate when the source is not present *[1 mark]*. Subtract the background count rate from the source count rate to get the corrected count rate *[1 mark]*.

p.68 — Medical Uses of Ionising Radiation
Q1 Gamma emitting radioactive isotopes are swallowed by or injected into a person's body *[1 mark]*. The gamma radiation emitted by the isotope is detected outside of the body by a radiation detector *[1 mark]*.

Q2 Gamma rays are directed at a tumour from outside of the body *[1 mark]*. The gamma rays penetrate the patient's body and kill the cancerous cells *[1 mark]*.

p.69 — More Uses of Ionising Radiation
Q1 A long half-life means the source doesn't have to be replaced often *[1 mark]*.

p.70 — Background Radiation and Risk
Q1 E.g. radiation can cause cells to become cancerous / radiation can kill cells completely *[1 mark]*.

p.71 — Radiation Dose
Q1 $D = E \div m$ *[1 mark]*
$= 0.50 \div 0.25$ *[1 mark]*
$= 2.0$ Gy *[1 mark]*

p.72 — Comparing Radiation Dose
Q1 Annual effective dose limit = 20 mSv *[1 mark]*.
$20 \div 0.08$ *[1 mark]* $= 250$ days *[1 mark]*.

p.73 — Nuclear Fission
Q1

[3 marks for a labelled diagram — 1 mark for showing a neutron being absorbed to cause splitting, 1 mark for a large nucleus splitting into two smaller nuclei, 1 mark for it producing a neutron that is absorbed by another large, unstable nucleus.]

p.74 — Nuclear Fusion
Q1 E.g. nuclear fusion needs very high temperatures/pressures to occur / it is difficult to contain hot plasma *[1 mark]*.

Index

A
ablation heat shields 34
absolute zero 50
absorbed dose 71
absorption spectra 31
acceleration 16
  and force 20
  measuring 17
  on a v-t graph 18
accuracy 6
activity (of a source) 66
aims 4, 11
air resistance 23, 25
alpha particles 65, 68, 70
alternating current (a.c.) 47
altitude 32
ammeters 40, 78
amplitude 58
angle of incidence 61
angle of refraction 61
anomalous results 6-8
area under a graph 18
asteroids 29
atomic number 65
average acceleration 16
averages 7
average speed/velocity 15
  measuring 17

B
background radiation 67, 70, 72
bar charts 8
batteries 47
bearings 13
beta particles 65, 68-70
bias 3
Big Bang theory 30
bipolar (npn) transistors 46
boiling 52
Bourdon gauges 77
Boyle's Law 54
Brownian motion 50

C
cancer 63, 68, 70
capacitors 42
carbon dating 69
Celsius 50
chain reactions 73
changes of state 52
charge carriers 38
charge (electric) 37, 38
  storage of 42
Charles' Law 56
circuits 38-46
circuit symbols 38, 78
COBE 30
conclusions 11
condensing 52

conductors 38
conservation of energy 24, 25, 51
contact forces 19
continuous spectra 31
control variables 5
converting units 10
corrected count rate 67
correlations 8, 11
cosmic microwave background (CMB) 30
cosmic rays 33, 70
count rate 66
current 38-40
  measuring 46, 77
  parallel circuits 44
  series circuits 43

D
data
  collecting 6
  processing 7-9
  types 8
deceleration 16
  on a v-t graph 18
dependent variables 5
designing investigations 4, 5
detectors of EM radiation 62, 63
diffraction 60
diodes 40, 41
direct current (d.c.) 47
direct proportion 22
displacement 13, 15
  on a v-t graph 18
distance 13, 15, 18
dose (radiation) 71, 72
drag 23, 25

E
effective dose 72
electric charge 37, 38
  storage of 42
electric fields 37
electricity 37-48
electromagnetic spectrum 61
electromagnetic waves 61-63
electrons 38
emission spectra 31
energy
  absorbed dose 71
  conservation of 24, 25, 51
  gravitational potential 25
  heat (thermal) 50-52
  in circuits 48
  in waves 58
  kinetic 25
  of particles 50
  released by fission 73
  released by fusion 74
  transfer 24, 25

equilibrium 19, 21
equivalent dose 71, 72
equivalent dose rate 72
errors 6, 12
evaluations 12
evaporation 52
experiments 4-9, 11, 12
  collecting data 6
  conclusions 11
  designing 4, 5
  evaluations 12
  processing data 7-9

F
field lines 37
filament lamps 40
fission 73
fluorescence 63
forces 19-24
  between particles 50
  contact 19
  frictional 23
  gravitational 22
  in electric fields 37
  in space 35
  Newton's Laws 20, 21, 35
  non-contact 19
  pressure 53
  reaction 19, 21, 35
  resultant 19, 20, 24
  weight 22
frame rate 17
free body force diagrams 19
free fall 23, 25
freezing 52
frequency 47, 58
  of EM waves 61
friction 23
  calculations 24
fuses 48
fusion 74

G
galaxies 29
gamma rays 61, 63, 65, 68-70
gas laws 54-56
  Boyle's Law 54
  Charles's Law 56
  Gay-Lussac's Law 55
  ideal gas equation 56
gas syringes 77
Gay-Lussac's Law 55
Geiger-Müller tube 66
geostationary satellites 32
graphs 8, 9
  gradients 9
  lines of best fit 8
  velocity-time 18
gravitational catapults 34

gravitational fields 22, 25, 35
gravitational field strength 16, 22, 25, 35
gravitational potential energy 25

H
half-life 66, 67
hazards 4, 77
heat (thermal) energy 50-52
heat shields 34
heat transfer 50, 51
hypotheses 2, 4

I
ideal gas equation 56
independent variables 5
infrared radiation 61, 62
instantaneous speed/ velocity 15
  measuring 17
insulators (electrical) 38
interaction pairs 19, 21
International Space Station (ISS) 32-34
investigations (see experiments) 4-9, 11, 12
ion drives 34
ionising radiation 65
  alpha 65, 68, 70
  background 67, 70, 72
  beta 65, 68-70
  dangers 70-72
  dose 71, 72
  gamma 65, 68-70
  medical uses 68
  uses 65, 68, 69
isotopes 65
I-V graphs 40

K
Kelvin scale 50
kinetic energy 24, 25
kinetic model 50, 53-56

L
leak detection 69
light dependent resistors (LDRs) 41, 45, 46
light emitting diodes (LEDs) 41, 63
light gates 17, 20, 77
light years 29
line graphs 8
lines of best fit 8
line spectra 31
longitudinal waves 58
loudspeakers 42, 46

M

mains electricity 47
mass 22
  measuring 76
mass number 65
matter 50-56
mean (average) 7
median 7
medical tracers 63, 68
melting 52
Mexican waves 58
microphones 42
microwaves 60-62
Milky Way 29
mode 7
moons 29
MOSFET transistors 46
motors 42
multimeters 78

N

n-channel enhancement
      mode MOSFET 46
Newton's Laws
  First Law 20
  Second Law 20, 35
  Third Law 21, 35
non-contact forces 19
npn transistors 46
nuclear fission 73
nuclear fusion 74
nuclear power stations 73

O

Ohm's Law 39, 40
optical fibres 63
orbital periods 32
oscilloscopes 47, 59

P

parachutes 23
parallax (in measurements) 76
parallel circuits 44
period (of a wave) 58
photovoltaic (solar) cells
      33, 41
planets 29
plasma 74
potential difference 38-40, 45
  measuring 40, 78
  parallel circuits 44
  series circuits 43
potential dividers 45
power 48, 51
power ratings 48
precision 6
pressure 53
  in gases 53-56, 77
  differential (in space) 33
  gauges 77
projectile motion 26, 27
Pythagoras 14

R

radiation (see ionising
      radiation) 65-72
radioactive decay 66
radio signals 60, 62
radio telescopes 30
radiotherapy 68
radio waves 30, 60-62
random errors 6
ray diagrams 61
reaction forces 21, 35
re-entry (spacecraft) 34
refraction 61
relays (in circuits) 42
reliability 5, 6
repeatability 5, 6
reproducibility 5, 6
resistance (air) 23, 35
resistance (electrical)
      39-41, 45
  parallel circuits 44
  series circuits 43
  temperature 39
resolution 6, 12
resultant forces 19, 20, 24
resultant vectors 14
rockets (see spacecraft) 33-35

S

safety in experiments 4, 77
satellites
  as projectiles 27
  geostationary 32
  in the Solar System 29
  orbital periods 32
  uses 30, 32
scalars 13
scale drawings 14
scatter graphs 8
scientific method 2, 3
scientific notation 7
sensing circuits 45, 46
series circuits 43
SETI 30
significant figures 7
S.I. units 10
skydivers 23
solar cells 33, 41
Solar System 29
space 29-35
spacecraft 33-35
  electricity production 33
  manoeuvring 34
  Newton's Laws 35
  propulsion 21, 35
  re-entry 34
  risks of space travel 33, 34
  take-off 35
specific heat capacity 51
specific latent heat 52
spectra 31
speed 13, 15
  measuring 17

speed of light 29, 61
speed-time graphs 18
standard form 7
stars 29
  spectra 31
states of matter 50, 52
streamlining 23
Sun 29
systematic errors 6

T

tables (of data) 7
telescopes 30
television signals 60, 62
temperature 50-52
  in gases 53, 55, 56
  measuring 76
terminal velocity 23
thermal energy 50-52
thermal imaging 62
thermistors 41, 45, 46, 62
thickness gauges 69
thrust 21, 35
time (measuring) 77
tracers 63, 68
transistors 46
transverse waves 58

U

ultraviolet 61, 63
uncertainties 12
uniform acceleration 16
units 10
universe 29-31
unstable isotopes 65

V

validity 5
variables 5
vectors 13, 14
velocity 13, 15
  change in 16
  measuring 17
  terminal 23
velocity-time (v-t) graphs 18
  for projectiles 27
  for terminal velocity 23
video analysis (measuring
      motion) 17, 77
V-I graphs 40
visible light 61, 63
voltage 38-40, 45
  measuring 40, 78
  parallel circuits 44
  series circuits 43
voltmeters 40, 78
volume of gases 53, 54, 56

W

wavefronts 60, 61
wavelength 58
  measuring 59
  of EM waves 61
waves 58-63
  electromagnetic 61-63
  longitudinal 58
  transverse 58
wave speed 59, 61
weight 22
  on different planets 35
work done 24

X

X-rays 61, 63

Z

zero errors 6

Index